The Renaissance of Tibetan Civilization

Christoph von Fürer-Haimendorf

Foreword by
the Dalai Lama

Essay on Bön by
Per Kværne

SYNERGETIC PRESS

ACKNOWLEDGEMENTS

Grateful acknowledgement for their assistance is due to the Office of Tibet in New York, Thubten Samphel and the Information Office of the Central Tibetan Secretariat in Dharamsala, India, Paljor Thondup of Project Tibet in Santa Fe, New Mexico, Chojor Radha and Khanpo Karthar Rinpoche with the Karma Triyana Dharmachakra monastery in Woodstock, New York, Khanpo Konchog Gyaltsen Rinpoche of the Drikung Meditation Center in Washington D.C., Lobsang Lalungpa, and Tony Blake. Appreciation for photographic contributions is gratefully extended to Alan Arora, Kim Yeshi, Pema Rabgay, Theodora McKenna, M.M. Evans, Marie Allen, Robert Hahn, Phil Hawes, and Krystyna Cech. Photographs not credited otherwise are by the author.

Published by Synergetic Press, Inc.
  Post Office Box 689
  Oracle, Arizona 85623

Editor: Kathleen A. Dyhr
Cover and book design by Kathleen A. Dyhr
Contributing editors: Margret Augustine and M.M. Evans
Front cover photograph by Alan Arora
Back cover photograph by Kim Yeshi

ISBN 0 907791 21 2
Library of Congress Catalog Card Number: 89-061485

Printed in the United States of America by Arizona Lithographers, Tucson

Table of Contents

His Holiness the Dalai Lama

THE DALAI LAMA

THEKCHEN CHOELING
McLEOD GANJ 176219
KANGRA DISTRICT
HIMACHAL PRADESH

Foreword

Christoph von Fürer-Haimendorf has made a sympathetic and thorough study of the social forces and unflagging determination which have enabled Tibetan refugees to maintain their national identity, rebuild their communities and re-establish their culture and its institutions in foreign lands. His book, *The Renaissance of Tibetan Civilization,* is welcome and will help to increase awareness of the remarkable achievements of the Tibetan people in exile following the tragedy that has taken place in their homeland.

July 26, 1989

i

Buddha statues at Swayambunath in Kathmandu

Preface

THROUGHOUT HUMAN HISTORY there occurred mass movements of whole populations driven from their homeland by invaders of superior military power. Different from such migrations were the flights of individuals unwilling to live under regimes imposing unacceptable ideologies on the vanquished. Both types of expatriates are referred to as refugees, but this blanket term disguises the fact that there are very different ways in which such migrants may react to their displacement.

Departure from a familiar environment often results in loss of a population's cultural infrastructure and hence in the sudden transformation of its traditional lifestyle and worldview.

However, there are cases of people forced to leave their homeland who are able to preserve their cultural heritage and reconstruct in a foreign land not only their material environment, such as houses and types of settlements, but also the social and ideological system which provided the foundation for their cultural characteristics.

Such an exceptional development occurred in recent years when the people and ancient civilization of Tibet fell victim to an imperialistic power intent on destruction of the Tibetan religion and culture and on their replacement by a totally different system — a system having little in common with the historical background of Tibetan Buddhist civilization but rather having received its inspiration and leading political ideas from Western Marxism. Had it not been for the unshakable determination of Tibetans who sought and found refuge in neighbouring countries, Tibetan culture and religion might well have been wiped off the face of Asia, an event which would have brought about the destruction of a spiritual system whose roots reach into the remote past of Indian religiosity and philosophy.

Under the inspiring leadership of their traditional ruler and spiritual head, His Holiness the Dalai Lama, Tibetans of all classes who had succeeded in

1

escaping from the Chinese grip set about reconstructing the culture which had unfolded over centuries in Tibet, and had aroused the admiration of all those aware of its aesthetic and spiritual uniqueness.

In Nepal and India, Tibetan refugees found an environment suitable for the recreation of the monastic life which had been characteristic of the Tibetan social and religious system. The ability of homeless and impoverished groups of refugees to build and fund in foreign lands numerous monasteries of a remarkably high architectural standard and their success in developing viable monastic communities similar to those of Tibet is one of the miracles of the twentieth century. The purpose of this book is to provide an account of the fortunes of Tibetans from the moment when they crossed the Tibetan border and entered the Kingdom of Nepal to the time when they settled in monastic establishment in the Kathmandu Valley.

It must be emphasized, however, that this volume is designed not as a treatise on Tibetan Buddhism but as an analysis of the social forces which enabled the refugees to achieve the transfer of their cultural heritage from Tibet to regions beyond the borders of the historic realm of the Dalai Lama. Some chapters contain recollections of individuals who participated in the exodus from Tibet as well as in the establishment and development of communities in exile, but it must be remembered that many of those responsible for the rebirth of Tibetan Buddhist institutions in Nepal and India are no longer alive, and that it was therefore not possible to obtain their views on the social forces involved in the renaissance of Tibetan Buddhism in exile.

Although the future fortunes of Buddhism in Tibet cannot be predicted, there is good reason to assume that Buddhist communities in newly established monasteries in Nepal and India will serve as bulwarks in defense of Tibetan Buddhism against any efforts of China's communist rulers to prevent the revival of this great religion. For whatever restrictions on the practice and teaching of Buddhism may be imposed in Tibet, Buddhist doctrine and scholarship are now passed on from generation to generation by monks and novices leading a religious life in the numerous monasteries in Nepal and India.

Christoph von Fürer-Haimendorf
Professor Emeritus
School of Oriental and African Studies
University of London

Bottom right: Tibetan Autonomous Region as defined by the Chinese government in relation to pre-1959 boundaries of Tibet; both regions are designated as part of China at present.
Above: Tibetan Autonomous Region in relation to surrounding states.

Buddhist stupa overlooking Kathmandu from Swayambu hill

1

Buddhism in Nepal:
An Introduction

TIBETANS WHO ESCAPED the Chinese terror and, at the end of an exhausting trek, reached the broad Kathmandu Valley could already see from afar the sacred symbols of their ancestral faith. The gilded dome of a magnificent Buddhist shrine rose high above the crowded streets of Kathmandu on the hill of Swayambu, and the colossal bi-spherical shape of the sacred shrine of Bodhnath marked their approach to the city. The familiar shapes of these buildings and the throng of pilgrims circumambulating the *stupas* (Buddhist shrines) assured the refugees immediately of a welcome in a place rich in the imagery of Tibetan Buddhism.

The fugitives did not have to go as far as Kathmandu to encounter a familiar and emotionally reassuring atmosphere. Most had come upon *chorten* (Buddhist shrines), *mani*-walls (walls of prayer slates inscribed by pilgrims) and *gonpa* (Tibetan monasteries) soon after crossing the frontier of Nepal, for Tibetan-speaking communities had created all the outward patterns of Buddhist culture in these border highlands. Buddhist communities there, however diminutive, had access to the vast pool of Buddhist learning in the great monasteries of Tibet, and it was common practice for novices in gonpa situated on the Nepal side of the Himalayan mountain range to travel for study and initiation to Tibetan monasteries which could be reached by a few days journey. This connection, so useful to isolated Himalayan communities, was abruptly severed in 1959 when the Chinese military began its campaign of destruction aimed at all centres of religious life in Tibet.

The roles were now reversed. Tibetan lamas — fleeing from their monasteries which were largely reduced to ruins — moved into Nepal and sought shelter among Buddhist populations who had for generations relied upon them to educate their young men during early stages of their monastic careers.

Buddhism flourished in various parts of Nepal despite the fact that since the middle of the sixth century A.D. the core of Nepal has been ruled by Hindu kings. The first well documented dynasty in Nepal was that of the Licchavis, presumed to have come from Bihar in India, followed by other kings usually referred to as Thakuris, who were also Hindus and claimed descent from Indian ruling families. Contemporary evidence of the existence of Buddhist institutions in Nepal can be derived from Licchavi inscriptions of the period 464-800 A.D.

Hinduism and Buddhism appear to have coexisted in the Nepal Valley and, as John K. Locke[1] remarks, this situation was similar to that which prevailed in India during the age when Buddhism existed in many parts of the subcontinent in close spatial vicinity with Hindu civilization.

The Buddhism of the Newar cities of Nepal was tantric and hence very different from the Hinayana Buddhism of countries such as Burma and Thailand.[2] Performing Mahayana and Vajrayana rituals, the Newar Buddhists shared many ideas and practices with the Tibetan lamas, although they were anxious to retain their independent status and there was no formal merging of the two religions. However, we will see presently that nowadays Newar youths are joining Tibetan monasteries as novices.

John Locke emphasizes that, in the past, Newar Buddhism was embedded in a dominant Hindu society confined within a very small geographical area, and that in Nepal it flourished within the confines of the three small walled cities of Patan, Kathmandu and Bhaktapur. Today these restrictions have ceased to exist and there is increased contact between Newar and Tibetan Buddhists.

There is an old tradition of monastic life in Nepal, and the new Tibetan

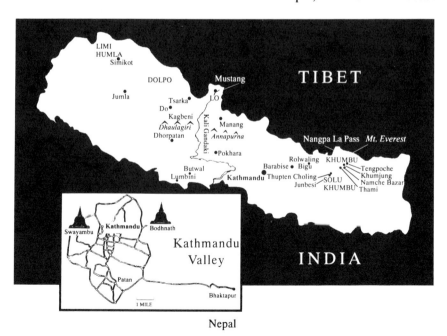

Nepal

monasteries conform to this tradition. *Viharas* (monasteries) in Nepal were built of brick and wood, but because of frequent earthquakes few vihara buildings predate the sixteenth century. Nevertheless, many remnants of Newar monasteries known as *baha* remain, consisting of a courtyard surrounded by residential buildings with a small Buddha shrine standing somewhere in the courtyard. These former monasteries, now largely inhabited by laymen, are very different from the newly built Tibetan monasteries but their very existence indicates that these new institutions are the last link of a long chain of monastic buildings, though no one will claim that this was an unbroken chain.

We know little about the internal structure of the Buddhist *sangha* (Buddhist community) in Nepal except that the Chinese pilgrim Hiuen Tsang mentioned the existence of about two thousand monks studying both Mahayana and Hinayana Buddhism. Temples of the Hindu gods and Buddhist monasteries existed side by side. According to Tibetan records at this time (circa 982-3 A.D.), many Tibetans went to Nepal and India for studies, and the *Blue Annals*[3] speak of pandits and tantric scholars under whom Tibetans studied. Among them was the famous Tibetan scholarly saint Milarepa, and in the early thirteenth century the Tibetan translator Dharmasvamin spent several years in Nepal at the vihara at Swayambu in Kathmandu. The last of the famous Indian pandits came to Tibet in the fifteenth century, after spending several years in Nepal where he later returned.

By the late fifteenth century the number of monasteries in Nepal had grown

Chorten and prayer wall at Tsarang (Mustang)

to one hundred and twenty. Of these, forty-four still exist as buildings though they are no longer used for ritual or even residential purposes.

John Locke remarks that, strangely, Newar tradition has not retained any memory of these Tibetan scholars whose doings are reflected in Tibetan sources. In his opinion it is doubtful at what time celibate monks disappeared from the baha of the Kathmandu Valley. Mary Shepherd Slusser[4] has expressed the view that there were celibate Newar monks in the valley up to the seventeenth century, many of whom — having been Udaya (persons of mixed Newar and Tibetan parentage) — existed right up to recent days.

While commentators are not agreed on the precise period when monasteries with celibate Buddhist monks disappeared from the scene in the Kathmandu Valley, there can be no doubt that there was never an overlap of such Newar institutions and the monasteries for celibate monks established by Tibetan lamas in the twentieth century. This does not mean that Newar Buddhism had faded out long before the Buddhist renaissance brought about in recent years by Tibetans settling in Nepal. Newar priests *(Vajracaryas)* have continued to perform tantric rituals right up to the present day, and there was thus a meeting of different Buddhist traditions when Tibetan monks and lamas flooded the Kathmandu Valley in their attempt to re-establish Tibetan Buddhist culture and religion outside the borders of their lost homeland.

Whereas monastic life and practice had declined in the Kathmandu Valley — the erstwhile centre of Buddhist civilization — when the extinction of Buddhism in north India had deprived them of all sources of renewal, the situation in the Tibet-Nepal borderlands had been quite different. Tibetans and border populations of Nepal could maintain more or less continuous interchange in those few regions where the Himalayan mountain passes permitted accessible travel. Regions where Tibetans and citizens of Nepal interacted most intensively include (listed from east to west) Walongchung, Chepa and other places in the Upper Arun Valley, Khumbu, Yolmo, Langtang, Kiron, parts of Nyeshang, Mustang, Dolpo, Mugu, Simikot, Limi and Yari. Notes on a few of these will suffice to exemplify the nature of the interrelations between Tibetans and Buddhist communities within Nepal.

Historical and contemporary documentation is most ample regarding the region of Khumbu in Nepal, which lies southwest of Mount Everest. According to local tradition and some documentary evidence, Khumbu was peopled by the Sherpas' ancestors who immigrated from Tibet across the Nangpa La pass some four hundred years ago. Several lamas of high status were among them, including the legendary Lama Sanga Dorje, who was regarded as a reincarnation of the Tibetan saint Chagna Dorje (Vajrapani). He founded the first gonpa in Khumbu, and his disciples and their successors have maintained gonpa in Pangboche and Thami. It took some time, however, before Tibetan type monasteries with communities of celibate lamas were firmly

Reincarnate abbot of Tengpoche monastery in his youth (1957)

Tengpoche monastery in Nepal

Thupten Choling monastery in Nepal

established in Khumbu. In 1923 a Sherpa of the village of Khumjung in Khumbu founded the monastery of Tengpoche, which has functioned as the focal point of Sherpa religious life ever since. The present abbot, the first reincarnation of the founder, studied in Tibetan monasteries and has developed as a leading figure among indigenous Buddhist clerics. Under his guidance, numerous Sherpas who had joined the monastery as novices rose to the status of fully initiated monks. In the 1960s, however, when the influx of foreign tourists disrupted social life in Khumbu, the number of monks declined and a shortage of trained lamas arose in most Sherpa villages. Even the major seasonal gonpa services proved difficult to perform without calling lamas from other villages to assist in the ritual.

At that time, as a result of the Chinese invasion of Tibet, numerous Tibetan lamas and particularly monks of Rongbo monastery in Tibet crossed the

Novice in the Tengpoche monastery in Khumbu, Nepal

Nangpa La pass into Nepal, seeking shelter in the houses of friends and acquaintances in Sherpa villages such as Khumjung and Thami.

Eight lamas resided in the twin villages of Khumjung-Kunde from 1953 to 1957. Several deaths among those of advanced age, however, left only two lamas capable of performing domestic and seasonal rituals in 1983. Fortunately for the villagers, six Tibetan lamas had by then settled in Kunde and they were most willing to fill the gap and officiate at any ceremony or rite to be performed in Kunde or Khumjung. In this way they assisted the local population and also earned a modest income by receiving the usual fees for their services.

The most impressive Tibetan settlement in Sherpa country lies some twenty miles to the south of Khumbu, within walking distance of the villages of Khumjung, Thami and Namche Bazar. This settlement is the monastery of Thupten Choling, founded in the 1960s by Thrulzhig Rinpoche, a reincarnate lama from Rongbo monastery located on the north side of Mount Everest in Tibet. When the monks of Rongbo heard of the devastation inflicted on Tibetan monasteries by the Chinese military, they decided to seek safety in the Kingdom of Nepal for themselves and the treasures of their gonpa. The border of Nepal was no great distance from Rongbo and they had close ties with many prominent Sherpas, making the plan to move as much as possible of their possessions across the frontier entirely practicable. Thirty sturdy yak were gathered and the monks packed up a large part of the library as well as many valuable paintings, ritual objects and a substantial amount of silver and gold. They knew they would need all that for building a new gonpa on Nepalese soil.

The reincarnate abbot and the monks crossed the Nangpa La with their

Novices at Thupten Choling monastery

treasure, and stayed for some time at the small Thami monastery where they were offered shelter and food. In search of a suitable site for a monastery, the abbot went to Chiwong in Solu where he had old contacts. Thrulzhig Rinpoche and his monks established a new gonpa at Singiphu, a high site near the substantial village of Junbesi. Singiphu proved too isolated, and they obtained permission to settle on lower land belonging to Junbesi where they constructed the Thupten Choling gonpa in the same style as their old Rongbo monastery, though very much smaller. Small houses were built on the steep hill slopes on both sides of the main gonpa building — the dwellings of monks on one side, with houses for the many nuns who had come with them on the other.

Several of the monks were experienced craftsmen, and the gonpa they constructed exemplifies the high artistic standard reached in many Tibetan monasteries. From a large courtyard, surrounded by buildings serving as living quarters and store-rooms, one ascends several steps to a porch with beautifully painted representations of the 'Guardians of the Four Quarters.' The walls in the main prayer hall *(dukhang)* are painted in a style equal or even superior to that of the best Sherpa painters. Walls and pillars are covered with gorgeous textiles originally brought from Rongbo in Tibet and lovingly matched with textiles purchased in Nepal.

The artistic quality of the Thupten Choling gonpa surpasses that of any Sherpa gonpa including the now famous Tengpoche, and it appears that exiled Tibetan lamas infused into the indigenous Buddhist societies of the Nepalese borderlands an artistic sophistication of which there had been little

'Guardians of the Four Quarters' painting at Thupten Choling monastery

trace before the sudden appearance of Tibetans among rustic and remote Buddhist communities there.

Soon after the foundation of the gonpa, the new monastery became an important centre of Buddhist teaching. Lay people and boy novices — from places as distant as Thami, Rolwaling and Thodung as well as from the nearby old monastery of Chiwong — gathered at Thupten Choling every year for lengthy ritual performances and prayer sessions. In addition, the reincarnate abbot Thrulzhig Rinpoche played a central role in the annual enactment of the *Mani-Rimdu* rites (Buddhist ritual with sacred masked dances by lamas) which nowadays are performed at the monastery of Chiwong above Paphlu in Solu. Although Chiwong has been the scene for the performance of the Mani-Rimdu for many years, the continuation of this practice was made possible only by the participation of Thrulzhig Rinpoche and supporting lamas of Thupten Choling. The present decimation of the monk-body of Chiwong made it impossible for that gonpa to enact the demanding Mani-Rimdu celebration without outside assistance, and in the whole of Solu Khumbu there is no indigenous lama of a status equal to that of Thrulzhig Rinpoche, who is recognized as a reincarnation of special holiness.

Solu is not the only region where the influence of Tibetan lamas has had a revitalizing effect on the religious life of the local Buddhist population. Several hundred miles further west, in the region of Upper Humla not far from the ancient Tibetan centre of Buddhist learning at Taklakot, the efforts of a single Tibetan reincarnate lama stimulated Buddhist religiosity in an area where there were few practising lamas and existing village gonpa were rapidly decaying. This lama, who did not seem to have a permanent attachment to any monastery in Tibet, appeared in Humla in the 1960s. He was a young man of great self-confidence and eloquence who had been recognized as the reincarnation of a Tibetan lama. Persecution of Buddhism by the Chinese communists had driven him across the border into Nepal, where he had taken on the daunting task of stimulating the restoration of village gonpa and reviving Buddhist ritual among the *Bhotias* (a term for Tibetans living in Nepal) of Humla. When I met him in 1972 in the area of Yari and Kermi, he was organizing the rebuilding of the badly dilapidated gonpa of Munchu village. This gonpa had fallen into disrepair and no services were being held in it. The Tibetan *tulku* (reincarnate lama) prevailed upon the people of Munchu and the Bhotias of some neighbouring villages to repair the gonpa and construct a new roof.

On the day I arrived in Munchu, all statues and images had been removed from the gonpa and placed temporarily into a large tent. Two days later, when the roof repair was completed, the lama organized the solemn return of the statues and images to the gonpa and the performance of a rite of rededication. A substantial crowd of worshipers, including several lamas from villages of

the vicinity, had assembled and the ceremonies began with the circumambu-
lation of the gonpa by lamas and laymen carrying the statues — among them
a statue of Padmasambhava (the Indian tantric master, also called Guru
Rinpoche, who was invited to Tibet in the eighth century by the Tibetan king)
— as well as a number of sacred books which had been removed from the
gonpa. Lamas blowing conch shells and playing cymbals led a procession
around the gonpa and into the newly restored building. On a raised seat to
the left of the altar, the tulku presided over a rite to rededicate the gonpa,
while the lamas and a few nuns sat down on the floorboards for there were
as yet no seats or cushions.

A few members of the congregation walked once more around the gonpa
at the end of the ritual. Soon afterwards, work on the roof and whitewashing
the entrance hall resumed, while carpenters fixed window frames into a
newly built gallery. The tulku and the villagers explained that much work
remained, including a plan to renew the frescoes in the main prayer hall. A
painter from Limi, a locality close to the Tibetan border, would be employed
for this task and a collection would have to be organized to meet his fee.

In areas of northern Nepal where Buddhist civilization was firmly established, such as the whole region of Lo-Manthang (Mustang), there had been
regular and more or less permanent ties with Tibetan monasteries; these were
not sudden impacts on local communities, such as the activities of the single
missionary lama had been in Humla. Territories such as the principality of
Mustang — ruled by the Lo Gyalpo or Mustang Raja — were culturally, if

Rededication procession at the gonpa in Munchu, Nepal

not politically, part of Tibet and the presence of Buddhist institutions were a natural outcome of the historic situation.

Buddhist influence on Nepalese communities did not always come directly from Tibet for lamas from Bhutan also stimulated religious life among tribal populations of Nepal. One such case is that of a Drukpa lama from Bhutan who was instrumental in establishing a gonpa for nuns on Nepalese soil. The foundation of this gonpa at Bigu by a Kagyupa lama from Bhutan has been described in detail in my earlier works, hence only a brief summary is required here.[5,6]

A Drukpa lama called Ngawang Palden passed through the village of Bigu in Dolakha district in 1933. The Sherpa headman was so greatly impressed that he requested the lama to preside over the foundation of a gonpa for nuns, where widows and unmarried girls eager to lead a religious life could find shelter and inspiration. Ngawang Palden accepted the invitation and raised funds to construct the gonpa while the Sherpa headman provided a site close to the village and persuaded the villagers to give their labour free of charge. The news of the proposed foundation of a gonpa attracted a number of monks and nuns — partly Sherpa and partly Tamang — and they all helped with the collection of building material. Ngawang Palden recruited Bhutanese wood carvers and painters to work on the decoration of the gonpa. Apart from the prayer hall (dukhang) and a small house for Ngawang Palden, quarters sufficient to house about thirty to forty nuns were constructed. After the death of Ngawang Palden, a Tibetan lama born in Kham and trained in

Nuns at Bigu nunnery in Nepal

Sera monastery in Tibet took over the headship of the gonpa which continued to be a home for considerable numbers of nuns from Bigu and neighbouring villages.

Numerous Buddhist institutions in the northern borderlands of Nepal are partly or even entirely maintained by Tibetans. Thus in Phu, a small isolated village in a remote valley to the north of the Manang region situated at an altitude of close to 14,000 feet, there is a gonpa which now depends on a family of Tibetan immigrants for its upkeep and management.

In the compact cluster of Phu, where high houses stand tightly crowded together, there are two gonpas as well as small clan-chapels but no regular services are held and there are no lamas concentrating on the worship of deities represented by dusty images.

On the jagged crest of a bare mountain ridge at no great distance from the village, however, the buildings of a small gonpa overlook a narrow river valley. High stone steps lead from a walled courtyard to a place where one may find a young monk teaching a few small boys preparing to join the monastery as novices and who are struggling to cover their slates with Tibetan characters. The monk is the son of Sonam, the head lama in charge of the gonpa.

Lama Sonam was born in Kham, Tibet. In 1958, he crossed the Himalayas in the company of a large group of Drokpa nomads who did not stay for long in Phu but continued on to India to join other refugees. Lama Sonam was asked by the villagers of Phu to stay and occupy the vacant position of head

Highland village in eastern Nepal

lama in the Tashi gonpa. He had impressed them not so much by his religious competence, which was not considered remarkable, but by his accomplishment as an artist and painter. The frescoes which he had painted on the walls of the gonpa were indeed impressive.

The main factor, however, prompting the villagers to offer the headship of the gonpa to a Tibetan who did not even have the status of *gelong* (fully ordained monk) was his willingness to stay throughout the year at the gonpa and guard the movable objects which might be stolen if no lama were in residence during the harsh winter, when most villagers leave Phu with their cattle and move to settlements at lower altitudes. Lama Sonam was quite happy to stay with his wife and son at the gonpa, and said that he had never visited Muktinath or Mustang and only once had he been on pilgrimage to Bodhnath and other holy places near Kathmandu. Although Lama Sonam was not a great scholar, he served the purpose of maintaining a link with Tibetan cultural life and artistic traditions at a time when political events in Tibet prevented the people of Phu from ever visiting monasteries in nearby Tibet.

Until the Chinese occupation of Tibet, when most of the links between Tibetan religious institutions and Buddhist communities in Nepal were suddenly broken off, many Tibetan lamas chose to spend part of their lives in monasteries on Nepalese soil and the influence they exerted on Buddhist belief and practice in Nepal can hardly be overrated.

The successful settlement and integration of Tibetan refugees in Nepal has been facilitated by the long-standing Buddhist tradition and philosophy which for centuries permeated religious and social life among the dominant population of the Kathmandu Valley and later spread from Tibet to many borderlands inhabited by tribal people akin to the inhabitants of adjoining regions of Tibet.

NOTES

1. John K. Locke, *Buddhist Monasteries of Nepal* (Kathmandu, 1985).
2. Tantric, Mahayana and Hinayana Buddhism are discussed by His Holiness the 14th Dalai Lama and Jeffrey Hopkins, *Tantra in Tibet* (Ithaca, New York, 1987), and in concise overview by Stephen Batchelor, *The Tibet Guide* (London, 1987).
3. Ghö Lotsawa (George Roerick, ed. and trans.), *The Blue Annals*, Vol. I & II (Royal Asiatic Society of Bengal, 1949-53).
4. Mary Shepherd Slusser, *Nepal Mandala: A Cultural Study of the Kathmandu Valley* (Princeton, 1982): 274-80.
5. Christoph von Fürer-Haimendorf, "A Nunnery in Nepal," *Kailash, Volume* 4 (1976).
6. Christoph von Fürer-Haimendorf, *The Sherpas Transformed*, Chapter 9 (New Delhi, 1984).
   See also Christoph von Fürer-Haimendorf, "The Unique Features of Newar Buddhism," (Paper delivered at the Buddhist Heritage Symposium, School of Oriental and African Studies, London, 1985).

2

The Road into Exile

IN THE SPRING of 1962 the repercussions of the Chinese invasion of Tibet had begun to affect many of the northern border regions of Nepal, where trans-Himalayan trade had played an important economic role for generations. The valley of the Kali Gandaki in western Nepal was no exception, for along that river ran one of the major trade-routes linking the lowlands and middle ranges of Nepal with the high plateau of Tibet. Flanked by the snow-ranges of Dhaulagiri and Annapurna, this valley provided easy access to Lo-Manthang, the walled city in Mustang District close to the Tibetan border. Caravans of mules, carrier-sheep and goats brought Tibetan salt to Nepal where it was bartered for wheat, barley and rice which were then carried across an easy pass to Tibet.

This flow of an age-old trade so beneficial to the border populations of both countries was interrupted in 1962 by events to the north of the Himalayan ranges. Invaded by Chinese armies, Tibet was in turmoil and the only Tibetans to cross the Nepalese border were refugees and members of the sole remaining organized fighting forces consisting largely of Khampas, the legendary warrior tribesmen of the province of Kham in eastern Tibet.

In Thak Khola, the region drained by the Kali Gandaki, there were several concentrations of Khampas. On the whole they got on well with the local inhabitants, many of whom spoke Tibetan and shared the Khampas' Buddhist faith. Tibetan lamas had been instrumental in establishing gonpa and reviving Buddhist ritual in the recent past wherever there were shortages of lamas to carry on services in local temples.

Many of the Khampas were under military discipline and relied on supplies obtained by way of India and on air-drops organized by the United States for their maintenance. Because of the delicate political situation in that frontier region and the intention of the government of Nepal to play down the activities of Khampa forces on Nepalese territory, I avoided contact with these refugee soldiers camping in various parts of Thak Khola. This was not difficult because my party — consisting only of my wife and me, our Nepalese research assistant and a Tibetan-speaking Sherpa from Khumbu — was in no way conspicuous.

Tibetan Refugees in Dolpo

A different situation arose, however, when we undertook a tour to Dolpo, an area of high altitude in Nepal extending west of Thak Khola towards the Tibetan border. Dolpo is sparsely populated by Bhotias subsisting on the breeding of yak and sheep, and the cultivation of barley at altitudes up to 4,250 metres. Adjoining Tibet, Dolpo was directly affected by waves of Tibetan refugees fleeing the Chinese invaders of their country, and many of them had brought as much of their livestock with them as possible.

The effect of this influx of refugees became apparent in the first village of Dolpo which we reached after four days of journey through uninhabited mountain country and across passes of up to 5,800 metres. The village was Tsarka, and even before we saw it perched on a hill, we had passed skeletons of yak lying on barren pastures where the animals had died of starvation. The people of Tsarka explained that Tibetan refugees had brought so many yak and sheep with them that the pastures were soon overgrazed and there was not enough fodder for both local and Tibetan cattle. Marauding Khampas, who had slaughtered animals to survive, had added to the depletion of the Tsarka livestock. Whereas the villagers of Tsarka owned about five hundred yak a few years earlier, only ninety-six of their yak now remained.

Conditions were not much better in the village of Do, which lies in a broad valley separated from Tsarka by a pass of 5,550 metres altitude. In Do we were also told of difficulties created by the incursion of Tibetans and their livestock which competed with local cattle for pasture. A long and severe winter with heavy snowfall contributed to the loss of animals — in previous years the cattle-owners of Do could take their yak to nearby pastures in Tibet which were relatively free of snow, but Chinese occupation forces in Tibet did not permit these traditional seasonal migrations of herdsmen.

The Bhotias of Do encouraged us to visit a Tibetan refugee encampment near their village to see their condition with our own eyes. Led by a local man we climbed along the slopes of a side valley to a considerable altitude. A typical yak pasture with rocky cliffs loomed up before us, with two groups of tents at different altitudes in the distance. The people of the nearer tents were simple Tibetans similar to the many refugees we had met in Thak Khola, but several men of very different appearance strode out to meet us when we climbed to the higher settlement — tall men wearing fur-lined coats of dark colour and expensive leather boots. Their shirts were of silk or other fine material, and they wore their hair in two pigtails. As they greeted us by shaking hands we noticed that their hands were soft and delicate, clearly the hands of people who were not in the habit of doing manual work. The clean appearance of all the members of the group also stood in striking contrast to the grimy exterior of most local Bhotias. The women had rosy cheeks and one of them wore gorgeous coral beads and a magnificent silver belt with several pendants delicately worked in silver.

The tent into which we were ushered was furnished with beautiful carpets and saddle covers of superior quality. A brazier standing in the centre of the tent was fed continuously with yak dung cakes, and traditional Tibetan salted butter tea was served in porcelain cups on silver stands as soon as we were seated. This was all the more welcome as we had received no hospitality in the houses of the Dolpo people, an experience much in contrast to the generous reception by the Thakalis of the Kali Gandaki Valley as well as most Buddhist populations of Tibetan stock.

Our host, a man in his thirties, expressed pleasure at our coming and assured us that he and other Tibetans greatly appreciated the help given by Western countries, such as the Swiss Aid programme responsible for the establishment of several refugee camps in Nepal. He then began to tell us of his experiences since the flight of the Dalai Lama from Lhasa in 1959.

He and his family abandoned their house and possessions in Lhasa, the capital of Tibet, and set out on the long trek to Mustang with some livestock and portable valuables. From Mustang they entered Nepal. He had taken this decision when he heard of atrocities committed by the Chinese military throughout eastern Tibet, where monasteries had been gutted and many upper and middle class families totally eliminated. He mentioned accounts of eye-witnesses who had seen the torture and execution of innumerable monks.

Herdsmen with yak in eastern Nepal

In some places, elderly abbots had been tied to the tails of horses and dragged through the streets to the horror of unwilling onlookers.

On their flight from Lhasa they joined a body of refugees some three thousand men, women and children strong. Often they were attacked by the Chinese and came under rifle fire, but some armed Tibetans acted as a rear guard to defend the fleeing refugees. He and his family wore charms obtained from a lama which he believed protected them against Chinese bullets. Other refugees were wounded and all suffered great hardship, often having nothing to eat for several days.

Once they had reached Mustang they were safe and could obtain provisions. The Chinese were close to the border, however, so they sought refuge in Dolpo where they found pasture for their yak and sheep, paying the local owners of these grazing grounds half a rupee per yak and half a rupee for every six sheep.

Though out of immediate danger they were greatly worried about their future. They could not return to Tibet, and in Nepal they were gradually eating up such capital as they had been able to take with them and which consisted mainly of silver coins. Our host and his wife had been to India where they made contact with the Dalai Lama in Dharamsala. Unlike some Tibetans of high status, however, they did not settle in India for they felt responsible for their followers who had come with them and depended on their leadership as long as they were in Nepal. The number of yak and sheep which they had been able to bring with them was not sufficient for them to subsist as pastoral nomads, and they could not obtain enough wool to make a living by spinning and weaving as some members of their group had done when they first arrived in Mustang. Their only income source was the milk of some fifty sheep and goats, which they used for their own consumption and for producing butter, a marketable commodity in all border regions of Nepal.

While our host had been talking about his problems, the women of the family had prepared a meal and soon we were offered heaps of boiled mutton served on individual metal plates with gravy and red rice. The whole manner of entertainment, no less than our conversation, left us in no doubt that we were in the presence of people greatly superior in general style of living and refinement to the rather primitive and uncouth local Bhotias.

Our Tibetan host, though himself in a precarious position, offered to give any assistance we might require on our tour through the mountains of Dolpo. As we could combine the acceptance of his courteous offer with our wish to repay the hospitality we had received, I proposed to hire at a generous rate two horses and a man to look after them and ultimately return them to the Tibetan camp. The proposal was gladly accepted and we parted with many assurances of good will.

Refugees in Dhorpatan

On that June evening in 1962 we did not think that we would ever meet our hosts again. Yet, four years later we unexpectedly encountered them in Dhorpatan on the south side of Dhaulagiri as we made our way back from a long tour in Jumla.

The flags of a gonpa attracted our attention as we entered a settlement of Dhorpatan. The gonpa seemed an insignificant make-shift building but this impression changed quickly when some lamas invited us inside. The interior was a small hall with beautiful, expensive and dignified furnishings. There were carpets on the benches, and coloured blankets were draped on the walls along with some very fine Tibetan *thankas* (Buddhist scroll paintings) with surrounds embroidered in silk. A few small but valuable gilded figures stood on the altar as well as the usual silver cups for offerings and butter lamps made of brass. Tibetan liturgical books, each carefully wrapt up in a cloth, were piled to one side of the altar. It was remarkable that a small group of refugees could recreate the atmosphere of a Tibetan gonpa despite great economic difficulties.

A middle-aged lama referred to as tulku (reincarnate lama) was dressed in a gold embroidered gown, and his appearance certainly suggested wealth. We later heard that he personally owned numerous horses and donkeys used on trade routes leading to the south. Among a few less conspicuous *drawa* (monks) sat a middle-aged layman whose face seemed familiar. Had we not seen him in Dolpo in the Tibetan encampment near Do-Tarap? As we asked him, he recognized us and showed a quite touching pleasure at this renewed meeting. He said that he and his group had lost their original sheep and goats,

Buddhist shrine in Dhorpatan

but now had horses and were busy trading between Dhorpatan and the Terai. Their main anxiety was the insecurity of their position in Dhorpatan, for although they had come to some arrangement with the local *panchayat* (government council) they had no permanent right to the site on which their houses had been built.

After the lamas entertained us with excellent Tibetan tea and we had laid an offering on the altar, our friend insisted that we come to his house, a rectangular shack with stone walls and a gabled roof of planks which stood close to the gonpa. The interior arrangement suggested the adaptation of tent-life to a more permanent structure. Our host had aged not more than one might have expected during the four years since we had seen him, but his wife had undergone a shocking change. In 1962 she had been an outstandingly fair-skinned, almost 'rosy' young woman with a small child. She now seemed old and shrunken with wrinkled skin and drawn features, the child a rather thin boy of seven or eight. She told us sadly that she had never heard again of her older children who stayed behind in Tibet and hence were in Chinese hands. She still wore some valuable ornaments and it seemed the couple had been able to hold their own. Large piles of sacks filled with salt and grain lined the walls and indicated the owner's success as a trader. He was engaged in transporting Indian salt from Butwal to Dhorpatan and then selling it to nearby villages, particularly to Magars in the Maikot area.

The Swiss social workers who were supervising the refugee camp at Dhorpatan told us that Tibetan refugees of originally high status had begun to reassert themselves and had succeeded in collecting dependents with whose help they were building up their trade and animal husbandry. Even

Gonpa in Dhorpatan

Thakali lama from Mustang

men who had been stripped of all their wealth and arrived in Nepal without any money had regained some of their superior economic status. Apart from the few Tibetans who had managed to set themselves up as independent traders, some two hundred and fifty refugees were being cared for by the Swiss Aid project. Their houses were built with the help of the Swiss and they were cultivating land allotted to them under the terms of the project. They still received some provisions but were encouraged to become more and more independent.

Khampa Guerrillas in Dolpo

After this diversion it is time to return to the narrative of our tour to Dolpo in 1962. We moved out of the inhabited part of Dolpo by crossing the Thiji La, a pass some 5,300 metres high, looking for a camp-site near the area known as Biling. The mountain sides — which had been brown and dry less than a month earlier — were now clad in fresh green and innumerable wildflowers had sprung up along with the new grass.

Approaching the Biling valley, we came upon two Khampas whom our guides took for sentries. As they saw us, they got up and started walking away in the direction of their camp. Dorje, our Sherpa interpreter, hailed them in Tibetan. Reassured by his speech and appearance, they turned and approached us. We explained that we were looking for a camp-site where we would find water — the only nearby spring had dried up and our Bhotia guides went to search for another source. We followed the two Khampas but before we could reach their camp, several other Khampas walked up the steep slope to meet us. One was an elderly man with short hair. Two others, who wore their hair in pigtails, were rather elegant young men in good new shirts and dark slacks. They seemed anxious that we not go to their camp and pretended that they had come to meet us in order to save us the long trek to the camp. They said that they had stayed in this camp a little more than a month after having spent the winter in a village of the Kali Gandaki Valley. Unlike other refugees who entered Nepal at Mustang, these Khampas had come to Nepal via Kalimpong.

Gradually several more men walked from the camp to join our group, including a charming old man with his grey hair cropped short, and a pleasant open smile. He had two large dogs with him whom he treated with obvious affection. He told us that he had been a monk in a monastery in Lhasa but had left monastic life and gotten married. When the Chinese invaded Tibet, fighting broke out throughout the country. He and his Khampa friends left their wives and children behind and headed for Nepal, fighting the Chinese wherever they could attack a unit with any chance of success. They were all worried about their families and could not enjoy food or drink, nor find peace in sleep. He asked whether we could give him some medicine for a toothache. When my wife produced her medicine bag, more and more Khampas

Khampa tribesman from Tibet

gathered, asking for medicines for all sort of troubles from headaches and stomach disorders to pains in arms and legs, and a variety of skin afflictions. It was pathetic to listen to the complaints of these men living in skimpy canvas shelters in the icy climate of the high Himalayas where even we, in our down sleeping sacks and feather jackets, suffered from the cold during the long nights.

But these men — cut off from their homes and families, with no hope of ever being able to return — must have suffered even more from psychological isolation. Most were entirely pessimistic and said they had only the one wish of killing as many Chinese as possible. Most of them had witnessed atrocities committed by Chinese troops in the villages and monasteries of Kham, where men, women and children of all families apparently belonging to the landowning class or the intellectual elite were killed, and artillery was used to destroy monasteries with all their art treasures and large libraries of religious scriptures. They could not understand the fury unleashed by the Chinese on the peaceful people of Tibet who only wanted to be left alone to farm their land and maintain their religious traditions and practices.

Most of those crowding around us seemed to be simple men caught up in a situation they could not fully understand and had no means of influencing. They were certainly not the members of a well trained fighting force but rather appeared to be a rabble of young and middle-aged men from various walks of life, bewildered by the necessity of hiding in these remote mountains. Like most Tibetans they were extremely courteous and greatly appreciative of the few medicines we could give them. Only one of them spoke some Nepali, which he had learnt in Kalimpong after leaving Tibet. He explained that they were not short of food but got regular rations of rice, wheat flour and Tibetan tea, and occasionally some cash to buy meat. Their funds came from the Dalai Lama's organization, reaching them through a chain of officials stationed in India and Nepal where supplies and cash passed through Pokhara and then filtered up through the Kali Gandaki Valley.

A few days later we reached Kagbeni, a large Bhotia village on the banks of the Kali Gandaki River where Khampas occupied many of the local houses. Some of these were used to store provisions and firewood, and we realized that Kagbeni served as a depot from which outlying Khampa camps were provisioned. A caravan of mules had just arrived from Pokhara and we saw dozens of grain-bags being stored in one of the houses.

The Khampas and the local Bhotias were on terms of easy familiarity, and in an inn where we refreshed ourselves with cups of *chang* (Tibetan barley beer) we watched young women joking happily with several Khampa youths. The local men did not seem to object to the advances of the military Khampas to their womenfolk, and it would seem that only in a polyandrous society with a flexible sexual code could the presence of so many unattached young men fail to cause some friction. Years later when most of the Khampas had to move to India, it became clear that there had been a good many semi-marital unions of local women with Khampas. Such couples had the choice of leaving for India or settling in Nepal with the Khampa men accepting Nepalese nationality.

The departure of the military Khampas from Nepal was not entirely voluntary. In the 1960s both India and the United States had secretly supported the Tibetan resistance fighters with funds, provisions and arms. When the United States sought a rapprochement with China in 1971, however, the Central Intelligence Agency (CIA) suddenly cut off aid to the Khampa guerrillas. Though generously supporting Tibetan refugees on her own territory, India could not maintain the provisioning which had kept Khampa cadres in Nepal supplied with food and cash. The Nepalese government had long been under Chinese pressure and, when the two great powers withdrew support from the Khampas, had no choice but to rid its territory of armed forces hostile to China.

The Khampas were offered Nepalese nationality and rehabilitation assistance on the order of half a million dollars and the right to such land as they were already cultivating, but His Majesty's Government of Nepal insisted on surrender of arms. Some Khampas accepted these terms and remained in Nepal, settling in the border regions or establishing themselves in or near Kathmandu. The majority moved to India where they were given asylum and facilities for resettlement as exemplified by the successful Tibetan colonies in south India.

Tibetan refugee camp in south India

29

3

Conditions inside Tibet

THE REASONS FOR the continuing flood of Tibetan refugees seeking asylum in India and Nepal can be deduced from the interviews of high ranking lamas in Chapter 9 and the many personal accounts of Tibetan refugees. Independent sources also illustrate the conditions inside Tibet which caused a large part of the population to escape to Nepal and India. One of these sources is the "Letter from Tibet" by Alexandra E. George, a well known journalist and author of the book *Social Ferment in India* (London, 1986). She had visited Tibet in the 1960s and her letter dated Dharamsala, September 28, 1981 was published in the journal *Quadrant* (November, 1981). The following quotations convey the gist of the letter.

> A significant film came out of Tibet recently. Telling shots taken by the first of the Dalai Lama's delegations sent to ascertain the condition of the Tibetan people revealed thousands of Tibetans thronging the approaches and the courtyard of the Jokhang, the central shrine of Lhasa. Foreheads were pressed against the window panes of the delegates' car and, as the delegates emerged, the crowds surged forward, trying to touch them out of reverence for the Dalai Lama whom they represented. Old women were sobbing in ecstasy, their faces lined with the tribulations of the last twenty years. Numerous voices shouted "Tibet is independent" and "Long live the Dalai Lama". This spontaneous and emotional welcome of all three delegations is a strong indication of the failure of the Chinese policy to obliterate the Tibetan spirit.
>
> The Chinese seemed non-plussed by the fervour and spontaneity of the welcome for they really believed that the Tibetans had forsaken their 'reactionary' thoughts and adopted Mao's 'scientific and progressive' outlook. The new Chinese policy backfired, demonstrating how out of touch the leaders in Peking are with the local sentiments. Had they known how much religious feeling still existed despite the repression and destruction during the Cultural Revolution one may doubt whether they would have invited the three delegations to visit Tibet, including Amdo and

Kham, the latter now each under separate Chinese provincial administrations.

It is not clear who initiated the delegations' visits, but sources close to the Dalai Lama believe that the Chinese took the initiative through the latter's elder brother who lives in Hong Kong. From the Chinese angle the Dalai Lama's return to Tibet is desirable in order to close the issue of Tibetan independence and to serve as a testimony of China's new moderation in its persistent attempts to lure Taiwan back to the Mainland. On his part the Dalai Lama had said he would consider returning to Tibet if "he was convinced that six million Tibetans are happy." The delegations were sent to make such an assessment. Eager to prove this the Chinese have intensified the liberalization.

The relaxation has helped a truer picture to emerge from several independent sources ... the reports of the three delegations and reports of expatriates permitted to visit relatives in Tibet.

These reports show the falseness of Chinese assertions of progress in Tibet since 1959. One would at least have expected the commune system to have improved material living, but every source stresses food shortages at least up to the recent liberalization. Prior to this each commune was burdened with innumerable taxes such as the 'war preparation' tax, the 'grain surplus' tax, the 'antifamine' tax. All these were deducted at the harvest and the balance divided according to individual work points.

In 1979, bad agricultural policies forced upon the Tibetans, together with bad weather, led to the worst crop failure in modern times. But despite this each Tibetan had to surrender at least one thousand pounds of grain as annual tax. The resultant rations were so meagre that people almost starved and had for three months to forage for roots and grasses. Many Tibetans told the third delegation that they had not seen a piece of meat in nine years. Most of the meat is in fact exported to China. Yet official Chinese statistics depict the people as well off. In the city of Dragyab in Kham the Chinese told the second delegation that each Tibetan received five hundred and fifty pounds of grain per person per year. But Tibetans in the town told them that the actual maximum was three hundred and fifty pounds per year which often had to support a family of two or three people.

Tibet's natural resources are being exploited on the classic colonial pattern. The eastern forests are being denuded to feed the lumber industry in China. While Tibetans, even pastoral nomads face shortages of butter and cheese, unheard of in earlier days, and when a kilo of butter is priced at two and a half dollars on the open market in Lhasa, the Ngapa dairy plant processes dried milk from the commune's taxes and exports it to Hong Kong. Raw wool sold at twenty-three U.S. cents by the Tibetan producer is bought back processed at approximately ten U.S. dollars. Meanwhile, woolen mills at Dartsedo and Nyitri manufacture blankets and cloth, priced beyond Tibetan means, for the export market. The factories are staffed almost entirely by Chinese, Tibetans being employed only in menial posts.

The third delegation sent to study education inside Tibet returned with a dismal picture. Even Chinese statistics for the Tibet Autonomous Region, with a population of 1.6 million, claimed only four hundred and fifty primary schools with seventeen thousand students, twenty-two high schools with two thousand students and four colleges with five hundred and sixty students. In addition there are supposed to be six thousand schools 'started by the people' which received Government grants and catered for a further two hundred thousand students.

Independent interviews with recent arrivals from Tibet confirm the Chinese educational propaganda as a sham. In the sixty-five Tibetan schools inspected only forty-four percent of students and thirty percent of teachers were Tibetan. After over twenty years of 'progressive' development not a single Tibetan graduate, let alone an engineer or managerial cadre, could be located. Even the Tibetans who were taken to China received only political indoctrination without any higher technical or academic education.

The worst aspect of the system is the denigration of Tibetan culture by the 'Greater Han Chauvinists'. Few Chinese, even teachers, have learnt Tibetan. Children from some rural areas tell how apart from helping in the harvest they are put on to long hours of construction work even after dark to the detriment of their studies. No wonder two hundred parents have recently braved reprisals against their families and possibly a life-long separation from their children to smuggle them out to the Tibetan Children's Village in Dharamsala for their better future.

Even the new religious freedom is strictly controlled. A person is expelled from his commune and his ration card confiscated if he goes on pilgrimages. The Second Delegation reports that the eighty-three truck-drivers who gave lifts to the ravaged monastery of Ganden to Tibetans on their way to meet this delegation had their permits confiscated. The only monastery permitted to accept novices is Tashi Lhumpo, the seat of the Panchen Lama ... An official *Basic Study Guide* dated April 1980 from Chamdo reiterates: "We have to stop religion" and forbids youngsters under eighteen being taught religion or taken to religious places.

The term 'liberalization' is a relative one and Chinese rule, if less brutal than before, is still totalitarian. For example, the slight relaxation in freedom of movement means only the right to move in one's commune, village or town, permits being required for leaving a place of residence. The one exception is Lhasa, which everyone may visit.

Yet these changes cannot obliterate the atrocities committed by the Chinese up to 1979. The Second Delegation states that the most wide-spread complaints are nervous disorders because of living in constant fear. Dr. T. Chodak confirms that most elderly people suffer from heart diseases due to the mental strain caused by the sessions of *thabzing*.

The thabzing is a 'class struggle' session held to make the accused confess his 'reactionary' thoughts or behaviour. During the most intensive ones the accused's relatives are forced to abuse violently, kick, spit at and beat the victim, otherwise the general audience are incited to do so. The thabzings began in 1959, but from 1965 onwards they were held regularly and went on till midnight.

When Dr. Chodak was imprisoned in the Chinese Military Prison in

Lhasa in 1959, he was subjected to three thabzings for his 'old, stubborn mind'. At the third he fainted and nearly died.

Thabzings created such fear in people's minds that many committed suicide. Tsering Wangchuk, who visited relatives in southern Tibet, was told that his wife's grandmother had committed suicide in 1974 because "she had been hounded over the years by successive thabzings and could not face any more."

Comments by Per Kværne

The dismal conditions of the Tibetans under Chinese rule described by Alexandra George are confirmed by the eminent Tibetologist Per Kværne in his contribution to *The World of Buddhism* (London, 1984).

> The Chinese have been utterly ruthless in their efforts to stamp out the influence of Buddhism in the Land of Snow. Monasteries have been systematically looted, turned into military barracks, or razed to the ground. Whole libraries and countless religious images have been wantonly destroyed. A large number of monks have been executed, often after public humiliation and appalling torture. Thousands have been imprisoned or sent to labour camps. The anti-religious campaign was particularly intense during three periods: in eastern Tibet (Kham and Amdo) from 1954-5 to 1959; in central and western Tibet in 1959 and 1960, and finally — by some accounts the most destructive campaign — during the years of the Cultural Revolution which was launched in Tibet in 1967. No one can measure the sum of human suffering which these attempts at eradicating the doctrine of the Buddha in Tibet have caused.

The exact number of monasteries destroyed is difficult to assess, but according to Tibetan sources six thousand five hundred monasteries existed in Tibet in 1950 before the destruction by Chinese began. The largest of these — such as Ganden, famous for the scholarship of its several thousand monks — were razed by Chinese Red Guards who used explosives to blow up prayer halls, libraries, sleeping quarters and hospitals. By 1979 only thirteen of these six thousand five hundred monasteries remained more or less intact. Recently about sixty monasteries were partially restored, but less than one third of the original buildings remain. Only one tenth of Ganden has been restored. Some minor gonpa are now being rebuilt or repaired by the local population, but this work is permitted only in their free time and in many areas people are too frightened to do even that. Moreover, only twenty-five monks are usually allowed to reside in a monastery, a number too small to keep the monastery in order, perform the traditional rituals, teach novices, and replace essential books which were removed by the Chinese. Some sacred texts hidden or buried underground in the 1950s and 1960s are now being retrieved and newly printed books produced in Dharamsala or Tibetan monasteries in south India are sometimes brought to Tibet by pilgrims.

Dupa Lodou in traditional Tibetan dress in Kathmandu, Nepal.

4

Tibetans in Kathmandu

MORE THAN TWENTY years after my encounters with Khampas and other Tibetans in Dolpo and Thak Khola, I met some of these Tibetans again in Kathmandu and learnt of their efforts to build a new existence in Nepal. The fortunes and present conditions of some individual personalities settled in the Kathmandu Valley exemplify the resilience and industry of Tibetans exiled from their homeland.

Dupa Lodou

Dupa Lodou was born in Dongpa Medma, one of twenty-five districts semi-autonomously ruled by the King of Nangchen in Kham in eastern Tibet. The son of the *lyonpo* (a cabinet minister) of Dongpa district, a social disposition inherited in the family through many generations, Dupa would have become a lyonpo after the death of his father had the Chinese not invaded Tibet. His *rhü* (clan) being Khoru, his family is known as Khoru-Tsang, meaning the family of Khoru heritage.

As a member of a high ranking family, his father married one of the daughters of the Gona-Tsang, the family of Paljor Thondup whose family legend goes far back in Tibetan history although exact dates are unknown. The oral history of the family tells that at one time two powerful families in a province of the Dongpa district governed most of the area, and that they were later joined by the Gona-Tsang family. These two families were known as Khetsa-Tsang and Tsabsar-Tsang. Instead of a power struggle between these large families, their sons and daughters inter-married. Thus united, they became more and more powerful. They shared their power and wealth, and attracted many more families of equal rank and rhü in that province. The population grew rapidly and they became the most powerful province of the entire Dongpa district. The province was later named 'Khetsab-Ngee', this name being composed of the first letters of the original families' names.

Although powerful and wealthy, these families remained honest, united and through generations maintained the trust of the people of their district.

In 1957, when Dupa was not quite ten years old, his parents fled Kham to avoid falling into the hands of the Chinese and sought refuge in Lhasa where Dupa stayed with them until 1959. His father fought against the invading Chinese, but later went with his family to Tsurpu Gonpa, a day and a half walk from Lhasa and the seat of the Karmapa Lama, the head of the Karma Kagyu school of Buddhism.

From Tsurpu they went to Yangbadzing where they joined a group of about three thousand men, women and children who were attempting to escape to Nepal and India. At the Nam Tso Lake they were surrounded by Chinese soldiers who trapped them between the great lake and the high range mountains of Ngachen Thangla. Outnumbered by the Chinese, the Tibetans lost all their supplies and had virtually no food for one week. Of the original three thousand Tibetan refugees, only sixty survived. Dupa and his family, including his mother who was wounded, were among the survivors although his father was killed later in their flight from Tibet.

Dupa and the remaining group reached Mustang in Nepal and camped outside the walled town of Lo-Manthang. Fifteen days later they were joined by another group of Tibetan refugees. Among them was Tsering Chodon, whose life history is recounted later in this chapter.

As Dupa grew up, Ato Rinpoche,* a friend of his late father, arranged for him and his cousin Paljor to go to a school in Dalhousie which was intended for the training of reincarnations. Neither of the boys was a tulku, but Ato Rinpoche's influence helped to get them accepted and they studied Buddhist scriptures as well as basic English language.

In 1966, with the help of an American friend, Dupa and Paljor were admitted to the Sri Aurobindo International Centre of Education in Pondicherry in south India where they finished high school. The two boys then separated once again, Dupa going to Nepal to help his mother who was very ill, and Paljor to England and later to the United States for further education.

Dupa's father had been a disciple of Sechu Rinpoche,* who also fled from Tibet and settled at Swayambunath. Dupa visited him and met Lutsip, whom he knew from the time they both stayed in Mustang. Lutsip invited him to stay in his house near the Hotel Vajra in Kathmandu and he accepted this invitation. In Lutsip's house Dupa had the opportunity to involve himself with the local Tibetan community and to revive contacts with refugees from Nangchen, some of whom he had known as a child. At that time weaving and carpet making were the main occupations of Tibetan refugees in the Kathmandu Valley and Dupa soon developed considerable skill as an entrepreneur in this industry.

*Ato Rinpoche's personal account of his life history is given in Chapter 9 and Sechu Rinpoche's history in Chapter 12. .

When I met him in 1984 he was managing a successful carpet-making workshop in which close to thirty men and women were employed. Unlike some Tibetans in Kathmandu who produced carpets mainly for sale to tourists, Dupa concentrated on export and dealt with purchasing agents from continental Europe who preferred subdued colours such as result from the use of vegetable dyes traditional in Tibetan carpet making.

Dupa did not rely on industrially produced yarn, but employed a great number of people to spin yarn — fifty Tibetans in addition to the majority of workers who were Tamangs, Magars, Gurungs and Rais (ethnic groups from Nepal). Many workers were the wives and children of soldiers serving in British and Indian Gurkha regiments, and to supervise the production Dupa frequently visited Pokhara where many of his workers lived.

In 1984 a shortage of the wool required for carpet making caused prices to rise steeply. The wool of Nepalese sheep is not suitable for this purpose and only Tibetan wool had been used in the past by Sherpas and other Bhotias for weaving material for their clothes. The Chinese restricted the export of Tibetan wool, and Dupa told me that such wool as could still be obtained from Tibet reached Nepal by various routes. Some came by the official motor-road via Barabise and smaller quantities by way of Mustang and Thak Khola, or Humla, Mugu and Jumla. He himself required about six tons of wool annually for his business. In 1983 he could obtain Tibetan wool at a price of ninety rupees per kilogram but by 1984 the price had risen to one hundred-fifty to one hundred-sixty rupees per kilogram, for the wool traders were in the habit of hoarding wool until the price went up.

Because of the shortage of Tibetan wool, Nepal imported some wool from

Hand loomed Tibetan carpet at Dupa Lodou's workshop in final stages of production

Scotland but usually not more than forty tons a year; at sixty rupees per kilogram it was cheaper than Tibetan wool.

Although Dupa lived among a community of people from Nangchen he had no close relatives in Kathmandu. His mother had died in Dhorpatan, and his only surviving sister lived in Dolpo. Like other Tibetans settled there, she came to stay for a short time with Dupa in Kathmandu about once a year.

Dupa's wife Panden Somo was from western Tibet, and had come to Nepal with a group of Tibetans who traveled via Manang. From there they had gone to Dhorpatan where refugees were cared for by Swiss Aid. In 1984 there were still about three hundred Tibetans in Dhorpatan maintaining themselves largely by the cultivation of barley, maize and potatoes. Some had horses and mules and engaged in trade with India.

At that time Dupa no longer lived in Lutsip's house but had taken over another house in the Bijeswari area of Kathmandu near the Hotel Vajra which he shared with several other Tibetans. He occupied the top floor with his wife, his mother-in-law and two school-going sons, while the second floor had been taken over by Bhuto, who was also from Kham and worked for Dupa as a carpet trimmer. The ground floor was occupied by Tsering Wangdi, who worked for the refugee centre at Dalup but had also a small carpet workshop of his own.

In addition, many visitors, mainly Khampas, came on shorter or longer visits. Sometimes as many as thirty guests from Dolpo, Tibet and India stayed in Dupa's house, all of whom had to be fed. Even rinpoches occasionally lodged with Dupa.

Paljor Thondup

Paljor Thondup, the son of a brother of Dupa's mother from the Gona-Tsang family, is approximately the same age as Dupa and they were often together as children. During the turmoil of the Chinese invasion, they were separated and escaped by different routes. Paljor was with a group of Khampas who fought their way from Tibet to Nepal losing most of their companions at the hands of the Chinese. Finally, his group joined that of his cousin Dupa just before reaching Nepal. They all went together to Mustang with the intention of attaching themselves to one of the Khampa guerrilla groups engaged in the resistance fighting against the Chinese occupation. Unfortunately, dissent broke out among the various groups and because of quarrels about the intents and purposes of the guerrilla warfare, Paljor's father refused to join the group that was aided by the CIA at that time.

Instead, his father and their group went to Dolpo and then Mugum where they frequently crossed the high Himalayan passes between Nepal and Tibet to intercept Chinese military supplies being transported by yak, mules and horses.

In the course of frequent combat with the Chinese, Paljor's father lost most of his able Khampa warriors, including his youngest brother Delshak who was only seventeen years old, and a close relative Namre Gadun and his son Kalsang who were very well known for their courage. Like Dupa's father who often used his swords to combat the Chinese when he ran out of ammunition, Namre and Kalsang killed many Chinese soldiers who were armed with automatic machine guns although they themselves were armed only with swords. At the Nam Tso Lake, in an encounter with the Chinese, Dupa's father with only three other Khampa friends — his cousin Lodur, Cheshu Dhadur and Sardak — killed one hundred and seventeen Chinese soldiers during approximately eight hours of fighting.

In early 1964, Paljor's father and some of his group members, camped together between a steep mountain and a large river, found themselves surrounded by guerrilla soldiers of another faction who sprayed them with an intense hail of bullets from their automatic assault rifles, sub-machine guns and hand grenades supplied by the CIA. Both of Paljor's parents were killed, along with two of his uncles, Dupa's grandfather and many others including women and children. The actual cause of this tragedy remains a mystery even today, but it was officially assumed to be a terrible mistake by the guerrillas in Mustang.

In 1964, Paljor — now the only surviving member of the entire Gona-Tsang family — went to Dhorpatan where he ran a horse trading business, which turned out to be rather lucrative. At the time, there were no other means of transportation except horses. Many Tibetan refugees settled in Dhorpatan were aided by the Swiss Red Cross whose supplies for the refugees had to be transported by horses. Paljor acquired some ten horses and a mule, and hired two Khampa friends who loaded and unloaded the horses which mainly carried food supplies for the refugees.

After spending some time in this rather isolated area of Nepal — with virtually no communications with the outside world except a few foreign visitors in a year — Paljor decided to go to India where most Tibetan refugees were living, including His Holiness the Dalai Lama and his government-in-exile in Dharamsala.

Driven by strong ambition to learn more about the world outside, from which he had been cut off in the past by Tibet's natural isolation, he and his cousin Dupa united once again and set out for India. With many difficulties — caused by the Indian wars in the early 1960s, first with China and then with Pakistan — they finally reached Dharamsala where the two boys were welcomed by people from their district of Nangchen and friends of their late fathers.

In spite of tremendous support received from their friends, life was not easy for them in Dharamsala because of great differences between their lives in Tibet and the new Indian environment. The boys spoke only Tibetan which found its use only within the Tibetan communities; their sole means of communication with Indians was hand gestures.

Their dream of being able to learn about and communicate with the outside world came true when they were admitted, first, to a school which was exclusively for lamas or tulkus and, later, to the Sri Aurobindo International Centre of Education in Pondicherry in south India where the two boys finished their high school education in 1973.

In 1974, Paljor went to England for further studies and from there to the United States with the help of a friend whom he met in England. He went to a college in Santa Fe, New Mexico while also working for a construction company there. In 1977, for the first time he returned to Nepal to initiate a joint venture by his American and Tibetan friends to build the Hotel Vajra in Kathmandu. While he was there, he helped his old friends Lochap, Tusam, Oga and many others in running a small carpet workshop with about a dozen weavers. With the help of American friends, he exported the carpets produced by his Tibetan friends to the United States where he marketed the carpets, sending the proceeds back to Kathmandu. In a few years, his friends' carpet factory — which started out with about a dozen workers — became one of the largest in the Kingdom of Nepal, with more than two hundred workers. Paljor then helped to set up a day care centre with qualified teachers at full salaries for the children of the factory employees, as well as a dispensary. Since then, he makes frequent visits to Nepal and India to supervise and assist these projects.

In 1979, Paljor launched Project Tibet, Inc. in the United States, again with

Paljor Thondup in his office at Project Tibet in Santa Fe, New Mexico

support from American friends. A non-profit organization dedicated to the preservation of Tibetan culture both in and outside Tibet, Project Tibet has grown into a successful Tibetan charity program and a centre for Tibetan culture and information.

Paljor has had many offers to serve within Tibetan communities as a leader, especially from various groups of his own district, which he has declined. He feels he can best serve the Tibetan cause from the United States and also, despite a deep devotion to his country and people, prefers not to be involved in politics.

Sangbo Lama

Sangbo Lama was born in the Nangchen district of Kham and is of the rhü Khungpa. The name 'Lama' is one he took when he came to Nepal. He left Tibet when he was five years old; his age in 1984 was unclear although he thought he was in his early thirties. His grandfather is reputed to have been a militant chief who so terrorized a district that he was given his own village to run. Sangbo crossed into Nepal in the Dolpo region and met up with Paljor Thondup's family group when he was six years old. His memories of escaping from Tibet were: one day fighting, one day relaxing and one day running. His group was involved in fighting all the way to the border. His memories of Dolpo included recollections of many Bönpo lamas with their hair in plaits and wrapped around their heads. In Dolpo they lived in large tents, supporting themselves by goats and yak which they had brought from Tibet. In the first few years there was considerable movement back and forth

Hotel Vajra in Bijeswari area of Kathmandu with the Swayambunath stupa in
background at the crest of the hill of Swayambu

across the border with people grazing their animals on the Tibet side. By 1962 the Dolpo region had been devastated by overgrazing.

Sangbo and his father went to Pokhara and tried to make their way to India but were hindered by a shortage of funds. They stayed in Pokhara where there were two refugee camps. Sangbo spent part of his childhood begging,

Sangbo Lama in Kathmandu

but later he became a taxi driver and finally the personal driver of General Wangdi, who was head of the Tibetan guerrilla force. When the guerrilla army was disbanded, he went back to driving a taxi in Kathmandu until he became involved in the Hotel Vajra construction in 1978. He worked his way up the ladder from errand runner to crew foreman, then labour foreman and then overall construction foreman. When construction was completed he moved into a management position in the hotel operations as technical manager, one of three policy making managers for Hotel Vajra. Although barely literate, his excellent memory and intuitive grasp of visuals soon enabled him to read architectural drawings and transmit them to the construction crews. He also acted as translator on the construction site for Tibetan and Nepali to English.

Sangbo and his father had been separated from his mother during their exodus from Tibet and his father later remarried. It was only in 1982 that Sangbo visited his mother who, as he had discovered, was still alive and was herself remarried and settled in Orissa in southeast India in Camp Three of the Tibetan Central Government. She and her new family were farming five or six acres in Chandragiri in the hills. Sangbo had not seen his mother for twenty years.

Tusam

Tusam, of Sin-nienda rhü, was about twenty years old when he came to Mustang. At seventeen he was fighting the Chinese in Tibet, largely with American guns dropped to the Khampas. Tusam's fortunes in Kathmandu were made when he brought four horses from Dhorpatan to Kathmandu in 1973 and attracted the attention of General Soshila Shamsher Rana, an uncle of King Mahendra, who bought one of the horses for two thousand rupees and engaged him as a riding instructor for his daughter.

Marie Allen

In 1984 Tusam shared a house in the Bijeswari area of Kathmandu with Tempo of Khepdza rhü, Oga, Sonam Tashi and the two sisters Tonka and Ola and Tsamba Loso, the son of Tonka's elder sister, who was a monk and went to school. Tonka's brother Garga also lived in the house as did Ola's mother Khando. They earned their living in different ways but all cooked and ate together, and at one time they employed a Tamang servant and subsequently a Chetri boy. Ola was a married woman, but her husband was in Tibet. He had spent sixteen years in Chinese prisons, but had recently been released. In 1983 Ola traveled to Tibet to see her husband and bring him to Nepal if possible. The Chinese, however, did not permit him to leave Tibet.

Tibetan Households in Bijeswari

Several households of Tibetans in the Bijeswari area of Kathmandu had originally lived in the same area of Kham and, after escaping from the Chinese at different times, found each other again in Nepal.

One house belongs to Sangbo, whose rhü from his father's side is Khungpa while from his grandmother he inherited membership of the Hor rhü. The ground floor of Sangbo's house was occupied by Atshe from Nangchen. Atshe went to Mustang in 1959 and then to India where he worked as a casual labourer. He and his wife Pema Lhamo, also from Nangchen, lived for fifteen years in Kulu and their three children were born there. They came to Kathmandu because of the presence of their kinsman Sonam Tashi and the possibility of making a living as weavers. A second family living on the ground floor of Sangbo's house was that of Sangtshung, an unmarried woman of about thirty-four and her twelve year old son Ngawang. She came from Namro near Kham, entering Nepal at Mustang. From there she went to Dhorpatan and then to Pokhara to a refugee camp maintained by Swiss Aid. In 1974 she came to Kathmandu and found work as a weaver.

Tsering Chophel and his wife and small daughter found room also on the ground floor. They had come from Tö near Mount Kailash in western Tibet and had no kinsmen in Kathmandu, but their skill as weavers made them acceptable to the group of Khampas.

Tibetan women weaving a carpet

The top floor was occupied by Punjik, who hailed from Kham, and his wife No-do whose original home was Nyenan in western Tibet. Punjik was in the same guerrilla unit as Tusam but worked now for an Indian carpet factory situated in the Kathmandu Valley. His wife No-do is also a weaver, but at one time worked with Sangpo in the Hotel Vajra, and later ran a tea shop.

Another part of the upper floor was occupied by Likso, who hailed from the same region of Kham as Tusam. He reached Nepal earlier than Tusam and served in one of the guerrilla units encamped in Mustang. His wife Pasang was the sister of Tashi Dawa, who was the brother-in-law of Sangpo. Likso worked as a carpet trimmer in the Himalayan Craft Centre where his wife also worked as a weaver. Before Likso moved into this accommodation, Pasang, Tashi Dawa and their mother lived together.

On the second floor of the same house, Lhote from Nangchen resided with his wife Gamtso and two adult sons. Lhote had been a monk in Tibet and entered Nepal at Mustang. Using his expertise in Buddhist ritual, he made a living by performing such rites as *tsog* and *kurim* (prayer intent upon gaining a practical benefit) for anyone willing to employ him. One son was unmarried and worked as a painter, while the second son was a weaver married to a Chetri girl who also made an income by weaving. Another couple from Nangchen also lived on the second floor — Nupal, a man of about fifty who worked as a carpet trimmer, and his wife who did weaving. Their eldest daughter was married to Tonka's brother, and the elder of two sons was a monk, while the younger one was only eight years old.

A nearby house was inhabited by Lobsang Thogme and his wife. His original home was Thai in Kham and he escaped from Tibet at the time of the Dalai Lama's flight and, like the latter, reached India via Bomdila. He was a monk in Goden Monastery and worked now as a carpet trimmer. His wife's home was in Tö and she came via Dolpo and Mustang. The couple met in Kathmandu and had two sons and one daughter. The wife worked as a weaver.

Not far away another house served as living quarters and also accommodated a carpentry shop. The inhabitants were Sherab and his wife Pemba. He came originally from Senchen Gonpa in Kham, which was also the home of Tusam, and he now worked as a carpet trimmer. His wife came from Tö in western Tibet and she worked as a weaver. They had three sons between the ages of seven and fifteen. Ngawang Phuntsog, who lived on the upper floor of the house, also came from Senchen Gonpa and his wife Sonam Lhatso hailed from Nangchen too. Both worked as weavers. Part of this floor was occupied by a couple of mixed origin. The husband, Sherap, is from Nangchen and worked as carpet trimmer, while his wife comes from Utsang near Lhasa and, being educated, taught in a small nursery school attached to the Himalayan Craft Centre.

The ground floor of the same house was occupied by Migyur from Tö. He reached Kathmandu via Mustang, and then married Trumso from Nangchen who had entered Nepal through Dolpo and had stayed for a long time in Dhorpatan. Migyur was an educated man and worked as accountant for the Himalayan Craft Centre, where his wife was a weaver.

A couple professing the Bn faith, Rigzin and Namgyal Sangmo, lived in a neighbouring house. The former hailed from a village in Kham. He and his wife had met in Dolpo, where it is likely they had learnt about the Bön religion, which is widespread among the local population and represented by a number of gonpa there. Rigzin and Namgyal Sangmo had three children — one son and two daughters. Yeshi, the elder daughter was married to Tashi Dawa. When she was only fifteen, she and Tashi Dawa eloped on the occasion of the Balaju 'picnic' and found shelter at Swayambunath in the house of a friend of Tashi Dawa. Rigzin, the girl's father, objected to the marriage because she was too young and he also did not like her marrying a non-Bönpo. Nevertheless a regular Tibetan wedding ceremony without any Bön rites legalized the elopement, and Yeshi's mother cooperated notwithstanding his disapproval of the match.

Tsering Chodon

Tsering Chodon of Dompa rhü hailed from Nangchen and traveled to Nepal in a group of three hundred people with her husband among them. Her native place was Ambonju, which is now called Dompa, the chief's name. Her father was chieftain of Ambonju and Dompa was his family name. Ambonju district is near the border of Kham in eastern Tibet about three days journey on horse-back from the home district of Dupa. Tsering married at the age of sixteen and was eighteen years old when she left Tibet.

Her husband was the *bekhu* or *ponpo* (chief or governor) of their home region. During their flight from Tibet her group was surrounded by Chinese forces and, as some of her companions escaped in one direction and some in other directions, they had lost contact with each other. In Lo-Manthang her group and that of Dupa had met again.

She and her husband came to Nepal in 1960, and stayed first at Lo-Manthang. In 1961 they both went to Dharamsala in India, where she found employment as a road worker at a wage of forty-five rupees per month. In Dharamsala she met Frieda Bedi, an English woman married to an Indian, who had become a Buddhist nun and spoke Tibetan. She befriended Tsering and when Tsering was twenty-one she arranged for her education at the ashram school of Aurobindo in Pondicherry. Instruction and board were free at this school and only the fare had to be paid by the English lady. Tsering's husband meanwhile stayed in the vicinity of Dharamsala and maintained himself by roadwork. In 1984 he was in the Tibetan settlement in Bir; despite their long separation, he and Tsering remained on good terms. While Tsering was in Pondicherry she arranged for Paljor and Dupa to go there and attend Aurobindo's school where they learnt English.

Later Tsering worked as a nurse in Mussoorie in northern India, the site of a large Tibetan refugee community, and from there went to Simla where she taught for three years in a nursery school for Tibetans which was financed by the Save the Children Fund. She later held a teaching position for two

Tsering Chodon with her daughter in Kathmandu

years in Clements Town near Dehra Dun in northern India. At the time of my visit to Kathmandu, Tsering was employed as the librarian of a great collection of Tibetan books at the Hotel Vajra.

Tibetans from eastern Tibet living in India, Nepal and Bhutan elected Tsering as a member of the Tibetan parliament in exile. She was elected for a second and third term, but did not complete the third term. She resigned her seat and went to Tibet on a private visit to see members of her family who had survived the Chinese massacres and executions. On this journey she was accompanied by Sotop, a disciple of Sechu Rinpoche, who had spent some time at Swayambunath. Both Sotop and Sechu Rinpoche were friends of her family and had often been in her parents' house before Kham was overrun by the Chinese. Some other lamas also accompanied her on her visit to Tibet.

In Kham they were enthusiastically received. The local Tibetan people crowded around them with mixed emotions and touched the lamas' clothes with the hope of being blessed. But Tsering and the lamas were always accompanied by Chinese guards who tried to prevent them from talking at ease with those who came to welcome them. They were taken on a sightseeing tour to Lhasa and shown some of the remaining monasteries. The gonpa in smaller localities were in ruins and they were told that the Chinese strictly controlled any repair work. Yet as soon as permission was given for the rebuilding of a gonpa, the local lay population started construction, often having collected materials before permission was obtained. Even when a monastery was restored, the Chinese did not allow more than fifteen monks to live in it. Monks who were forced to lead the life of farm workers circumvented this restriction by gathering in the gonpa at the time of festivals and participating in the rituals.

Tsering found some members of her family alive but in very reduced circumstances. The Chinese had limited cultivation and animal husbandry, and the greater part of the crops was requisitioned after harvest and sent to China. Tsering said that she was not attracted by the idea of returning to Tibet for good unless Tibet is declared free. Although some of the most oppressive Chinese controls had been relaxed, Tibetans did not trust Chinese promises, and Tsering herself was apprehensive regarding the future development of Chinese rule over Tibet. She remembered only too well that the Chinese had first promised to set up an autonomous government of Khampas in the Chando region and then made every effort to destroy the very foundations of Tibetan culture. They had shattered the traditional social structure by rounding up landowners and members of the intellectual elite, and executing all who opposed their drastic reforms. All religious beliefs and practices had been denounced as counter-revolutionary and monks had been tortured and killed.

Although in 1983 and 1984 the Chinese authorities in Tibet tried to persuade Tibetan refugees to return to Tibet, those settled in Nepal and India had heard so many eyewitness accounts of atrocities committed by the Chinese military against the civilian population of Tibet that attempts to induce refugees to return to their homeland were bound to fail.

Tenzin Choegyal

Tenzin Choegyal, owner of Nepal Carpet Enterprises and obviously a wealthy man, lived in a substantial modern house near Kamel Pokhari. His family had come from eastern Kham. In 1968, he and his parents went to Lhasa, and fled from Tibet to Sikkim a year later. While still an adolescent he worked in Kalimpong and afterwards in Darjeeling, India. In 1970 he obtained employment in Darjeeling and subsequently accepted a paid job in Kathmandu. By 1985 he had become an independent carpet manufacturer and trader. By then he had already spent a number of years in the United States studying at the universities of Cornell, Berkeley and Arizona. From the United States he returned to Nepal where he built up a flourishing business from scratch. When interviewed he emphasized that the majority of Tibetans in Nepal are doing well, which he attributed to their ability to work hard. Many are engaged in the carpet industry, others are shopkeepers or general traders, while only a few are engaged in tourism and in the restaurant business.

According to Tenzin Choegyal the Tibetan community in Kathmandu enjoys solid cohesion. There is competition in business but no factionalism. The majority of the Tibetans continue to be very religious, support monasteries and call lamas to perform rites in their houses. When monks are invited to read from sacred scriptures in a private house, the hosts provide them with meals and also pay them a fee, the greater part of which is passed on to their gonpa. The Tibetan community is largely endogamous. Intermarriage with Chetris and Newars is rare, and even marriages with such Buddhist people as Manangi and Sherpa are unusual.

Tenzin Choegyal ascribed the cohesion of the local Tibetans also to the leadership of the Dalai Lama. He himself had never been to any Tibetan settlements in Karnataka, and said that the Tibetans in Nepal did not maintain trade ties with Tibetans in south India or any distant settlements in other parts of India. It is usual, however, for wealthy Tibetans to visit Dharamsala now and then to pay their respect to the Dalai Lama.

Tenzin Choegyal described the relations between Tibetans and Nepalis as satisfactory. There was no hostility on the part of the Nepalis, though low paid government servants tended to regard the spectacular economic success of some Tibetan businessmen with mild jealousy.

Kim Yeshi

Tibetan students at study in monastery in India

5

The Dalai Lama's Administration and Refugee Society Structure

ALTHOUGH OBSERVATIONS among Tibetans of Kathmandu give a general impression of the refugees' lifestyle, a proper understanding of their situation becomes possible only when seen against the background of the administration set up by the Dalai Lama. A visit to Dharamsala in northern India in November 1985 enabled me to consult officials of the Information Office of the Central Tibetan Secretariat, and to gain thereby an idea of the general lines on which the administration of the thousands of refugees scattered over India and Nepal is being organized.

Most Indians refer to this organization simply as the Dalai Lama's Administration, but Tibetans see it as the continuation of the Government of Tibet as it existed in Lhasa before the Chinese occupation and regard it as the Tibetan Government-in-Exile. There is a Cabinet, the Kashag, with four ministers appointed by the Dalai Lama. In Tibet all executive powers were vested in the Kashag, and the cabinet is also the highest executive organ of the administration in exile. The Assembly of Tibetan People's Deputies was instituted in September 1960 as a kind of parliament. The Assembly consists of seventeen elected deputies representing the three provincial regions of Tibet — Amdo, Kham and U-Tsang (central Tibet) — as well as the five major religious sects, Nyingma, Kagyu, Sakya, Geluk and Bön. Conduct of the election, for which regional representatives of the Dalai Lama are responsible, is not easy given the wide dispersal of the refugees. Although there are no electoral roles in the Western sense, the people from the three regions and members of the religious sects are all entitled to give their votes. Any Tibetan who has attained the age of twenty-five has the right to contest the Assembly election which is held every three years.

Assembly deputies keep a check on the workings of the various departments, play an advisory administrative role by considering problems arising out of departmental work, and endeavour to promote a healthy relationship of mutual trust and confidence between the administration and the people. Their function as legislators cannot be carried out in practice because, unlike the erstwhile government of independent Tibet, the present administration in exile is not in a position to pass new legislation but can only act on the basis of traditional laws as they were recognized in independent Tibet.

Periodic inspection of refugee settlements, handicraft centres and schools is another important function of the deputies, and tours are undertaken to assess the overall conditions of refugees in areas such as Karnataka (south India), Arunachal Pradesh (northeast India), and Nepal.

The highest policy-making body of the Tibetan administration in exile is the National Working Committee, comprised of the seventeen elected Assembly deputies, the Cabinet ministers, and a representative from each major department of the administration. The Working Committee takes decisions by majority vote of the elected deputies present at the committee meeting. All important matters are then referred to the Dalai Lama for his approval.

Once a year a General Meeting is held, attended by the Cabinet ministers, the elected members of the Assembly of Deputies, the representatives of religious heads, staff members of the Central Tibetan Secretariat, Tibetan welfare officers, Tibetan settlement officers, and representatives of residential and day schools. The voices of various interests can thus be heard and constructive criticism of all branches of the administration discussed. This annual meeting lasts for more than one week and its resolutions are presented to the Dalai Lama for approval. The resolutions thereafter become binding for all the Tibetan establishment for that year.

The Dalai Lama's administration is concerned with more than the multitude of practical problems which arose from the movement of thousands of

Tibetan women at Tibetan Homes Foundation in Mussorie, India

refugees into a foreign land and their ultimate settlement in hundreds of camps and villages. Although the task of organizing new homes for a multitude of disoriented and largely helpless men, women and children was in itself a colossal achievement requiring sustained efforts extending over many years, the Tibetan leadership set itself even more ambitious goals.

The primary aim was the preservation and recreation of Tibetan culture and religion in areas outside occupied Tibet, where nearly all centres of Buddhist devotion and scholarship had been devastated by the Chinese invaders. In pursuance of this long term aim, the Dalai Lama and other religious leaders set up the Council for Religious and Cultural Affairs at Dharamsala. Its organization and purposes is officially described in *Tibetans in Exile,* a publication of the Information Office of the Central Tibetan Secretariat (Dharamsala, 1981):

> The Council for Religious and Cultural Affairs looks after the spiritual and cultural aspects of the Tibetan exiles, maintains close relations with the Buddhists of other countries, and encourages the preservation and dissemination of the Buddhist learning, thought and culture of Tibet. It also serves as an authoritative medium of information for those interested in Tibetan Buddhism and its historical development.
>
> Though the monasteries follow and practise the traditional religious rules and regulations, the monks of these monasteries are not merely engaged in religious knowledge and are given basic modern education. The monks also engage in manual labour in the construction of their own monasterial departments, quarters and agricultural work to support their monastic lives.
>
> In view of the enormous destruction of Buddhism in Tibet, the burning of scriptural texts, the banning of religious teachings and the devastation of monasteries and temples, the preservation of Buddhism among the Tibetans has become doubly important. This task is being done by the Council for Religious and Cultural Affairs. The Council supervises the religious education of young Tibetans.
>
> In the international arena, the Council for Religious and Cultural Affairs maintains close relations with other world Buddhist bodies and attends international Buddhist conferences.

The Dalai Lama's Administration maintains Offices of Tibet in the United States (New York), England (London), Japan (Tokyo), Switzerland (Zurich), and Nepal (Kathmandu) for purposes of maintaining cordial relations with the governments and people of the host countries, and to attend to the welfare of Tibetans settled there. By far the largest number of Tibetan expatriates live in India where their numbers are estimated at eighty thousand, and in Nepal with a Tibetan population of about fifteen thousand. In 1989, on the order of five to six thousand Tibetans resided outside the Indian subcontinent, with about fifteen hundred in Europe, and an estimated five hundred each in the United States and Canada.

Structural Elements of Tibetan Refugee Society

Tibetans now settled in Nepal and India do not form a tightly structured society but are a conglomerate of diverse elements accidentally thrown together as a result of the Chinese occupation of Tibet and the subsequent flight of thousands of Tibetans to neighbouring countries. Despite this heterogeneity of the Tibetan population in exile, these elements are held together by the feeling of a common national identity which is more strongly expressed by refugees in the diaspora than had been the case in Tibet before the inhabitants of the various regions were forcibly dispersed. This cohesion is strengthened by the universal loyalty to the Dalai Lama, who is the central symbol of both Tibetan ethnicity and Tibetan religion and culture. Both in Nepal and India there are communities composed of people from Lhasa and other towns of central Tibet, Khampas and other easterners, and also families from regions of western Tibet. Such people may originally have spoken different dialects, but co-residence and collaboration in many economic activities have led to the development of a common language largely based on the Lhasa dialect.

In our review of families settled in the area of Swayambunath and the Hotel Vajra, we have seen that men from Kham have married women from the area near Mount Kailash and Lake Manasarowar. Such marriages are still exceptions and there are no rigid rules determining the status of the children.

The few anthropologists who have analysed Tibetan society have emphasized the principle of lineal descent as a key to understanding Tibetan social structure. Research among some Tibetan-speaking people outside Tibet, such as the Sherpas of Nepal, has produced the notion that the main constituent elements of their society are clans and lineages perpetuated by patrilineal descent. This notion is confirmed by the character of the rhü (clan) which is an essential feature of Tibetan social organization such as found in the communities settled in the Kathmandu Valley. These people consider themselves as members of the same rhü to which their fathers belonged in Tibet. Rhü membership still determines an individual's social status. Some rhü are regarded as being inherently aristocratic, and rhü containing many lamas among their members also enjoy high social prestige. Conversely, the bad reputation of a single rhü member may cause a decline of status of the entire rhü, and a man committing a murder will spoil the reputation of the rhü to which he belongs.

Rhü are also the primary exogamous units, and rhü membership of individual men and women therefore determines their suitability as marriage partners. The chaos created by the flight and dispersal of families has resulted in a great deal of confusion, however, and many Tibetans are ignorant of the rhü to which their closest friends and associates belong. This confusion may also explain the fact that there may be people of different rhü in a large kin-group known as *non-thou,* consisting of interrelated families. Under exceptional circumstances one person can be a member of two different rhü — in a polyandrous society it is possible for a man to inherit the rhü membership of both husbands of his mother, presumably on the grounds that either of them may be his biological father. Among the Tibetans of Kathmandu, Lutsip was the son of such a polyandrous family; one of his mother's husbands was of Tshedig rhü and the other husband was of Kheta rhü. Lutsip was therefore entitled to membership in both these rhü. Such a situation is a rare occurrence, however, because in a polyandrous marriage both husbands are usually brothers and hence of the same rhü. The lack of clearly defined descent groups explains perhaps the importance of the units known as non-thou.

Another group of pragmatic relevance is the *thonje,* made up of a number of families who live in the same locality without belonging to the same rhü. The smallest social unit is known as *trongba,* corresponding to the nuclear family of such populations as the Sherpas.

Despite the leveling effect of the common fate of refugees fleeing their homeland, class distinctions have not been completely eradicated. Tibetan colonies in south India emphasize equality, but status differences continue to be remembered in communities in Nepal, perhaps because of the relative proximity of the refugees' home background.

The class of highest status is known as *ger-pa* or *ku-dr'ag,* and the class next in status as *ngag-pa.* The latter is a priestly class whose members are usually lamas. Though members of this class inherit their status, they have to acquire the knowledge necessary for performance of a lama's ritual functions by studying for a long time under a learned lama teacher. Ger-pa prefer to marry within their class, but if they cannot find a suitable bride they may marry a girl of ngag-pa class.

Below ger-pa and ngag-pa there is a class of commoners usually referred to as *miser* and among most Tibetan emigrants, such as those studied by Barbara Aziz in Solu, miser constitute the majority of the population. Low castes known as *ya-wa,* comparable to the Nepalese and Indian untouchables, are few in number and of minimal importance among Tibetan refugees.

The exogamy of rhü and the endogamy of classes, though still recognized as the norm, is not strictly observed in the heterogeneous refugee society, and marriage rules are also not always enforced. While in central Tibet there is a definite ban on cross-cousin marriage, it is tolerated among Khampas although not considered desirable; this attitude prevails also among the refugee communities in Nepal, which contain a large Khampa element.

There are nowadays a few marriages between Tibetans and Nepalese of Hindu castes. One of the sons of Lhote, an ex-monk from Nangchen, married a Chetri girl, who had been employed as a weaver in one of the Tibetan carpet workshops in Kathmandu.

Intermarriage between Tibetans and Newars settled in Lhasa was a well established practice and there was even an agreement between the Government of Nepal and the Dalai Lama's Government that daughters from such marriages were recognized as Tibetan nationals and expected to stay in Tibet, whereas sons were regarded as Nepalese. The Newars who concluded such marriages were largely of Uray (Katsara) caste and most of them specialized in trade with Tibet. Tibetan wives of such Urays moved to and fro between Tibet and Nepal, dressed like Tibetans and spoke the Lhasa dialect. Recently a young Tibetan refugee married an Uray girl of Kathmandu and there was a large wedding attended by Newars and Tibetans.

In the Tibetan settlements of south India there have so far been no marriages between Tibetans and Indians, probably due to fundamental differences between the life-styles of the two ethnic groups.

While villages and clusters of hamlets in Tibet function largely as corporate units for social and ritual purposes, such ready made units hardly exist among refugees dispersed over several localities. It is therefore not surprising that other groupings emerge spontaneously to provide the scattered refugees with a sense of cohesion and corporateness.

In Kathmandu this purpose is served by groups somewhat similar to the Newar *guthi* which combine for the celebration of certain festivals and the organization of a kind of picnic celebration linked with such festivals. Thus, a group known as Gawakitu comprises all the people from Nangchen who live in the Kathmandu Valley, and consists of about forty to fifty families. Gawakitu is the main town in Nangchen and gave its name to the picnic group.

Members of such a group hold a *thuktro* or picnic annually or bi-annually and there are two such picnic groups in Kathmandu. One is the Gawakitu picnic, the other the Dzendengombu picnic. The composition of such a group depends on the people's past domicile in Tibet, and not on their domicile in Nepal where they may live in different localities.

Some of the families residing near Hotel Vajra are part of a picnic group which also has members living at Dalu, others dwelling at Bodhnath and yet others staying in Jawalakhel in Nepal. The first picnic was held in 1975 with Tusam as one of the four organizers *(nyerpa)*. The organizers, who are appointed in rotation, collect money for the purchase of food and drink. The amount required may be as much as five hundred rupees, in addition to contributions in kind. This particular picnic is usually held at Balaju and lasts for three to four days. Men gamble and women play cards. It is also an occasion for romantic encounters and there are sometimes elopements during a picnic.

Some people who are not from the same locality in Tibet but know each other well in Kathmandu may join a picnic even though they do not belong to the regular group. Some such people are from central Tibet, but nevertheless mingle with Tibetans from Kham during the picnic.

There seem to be some parallels between these picnic groups and the ritual units *(kor-k'ong)* described by Barbara Aziz in her book *Tibetan Frontier Families* (Delhi, 1978). Each kor-k'ong is a cluster of hamlets with a special interaction through ritual service. Members of a kor-k'ong meet together at local festivals, exchange *tsog* offerings and jointly sponsor the local *lha-sol* (incense-burning ceremony to appease the local deities). Outside these rituals the kor-k'ong has no corporate existence or function, and in this respect these ritual units resemble picnic groups. The distribution of food by wealthy members of a kor-k'ong to all other members at festivals certainly has the effect of cementing the cohesion of such a group, and the providing and sharing of food and drink by members of a picnic group has the same purpose.

We thus see that, even in exile and totally unfamiliar surroundings, Tibetans from the same home-region tend to uphold their social cohesion by celebrating picnics of a semi-religious character.

The Care of Tibetan Refugees

Administrative arrangements for the care of refugees in Nepal are in the hands of the Representative of the Dalai Lama, who provided the following information. At the time of my visit, the Representative was Rinchen Darlo who later became the Dalai Lama's Representative in the New York Office of Tibet.

Situated in an old Rana palace, the Representative's office in Kathmandu is often besieged by groups of scruffy Tibetans who have just arrived in Kathmandu and are in need of accommodations. Many of them want to go to Dharamsala and need cash as well as advice for the journey. Each can get as much as one hundred rupees from the Dalai Lama's fund which is administered by the Dalai Lama's Representative.

From 1959 to 1962, about thirty thousand Tibetan refugees sought shelter in Nepal after escaping from Tibet across various passes. Virtually destitute, they were desperately in need of food, and with the view to keeping them alive the Dalai Lama contacted various organizations such as the United Nations, Swiss Aid, the Government of India, the Royal Government of Nepal and the Red Cross.

The first priority was the setting up of camps where the refugees could be provided with food and shelter. As soon as the Dalai Lama arrived in India, he established an office to deal with such emergencies and through which help to the refugees was channeled. In 1962 the Dalai Lama appointed an officer to investigate the situation of refugees in Nepal. The report of this officer explained that refugees were dispersed along remote border regions and some groups were exposed to near famine conditions, which had already resulted in numerous deaths. At that time the refugees had no means of communication among themselves or with the outside world. On the strength of this report, the International Committee of the Red Cross and the Swiss

Red Cross undertook the task of helping to rehabilitate the refugees in properly organized settlements and providing food, clothes and medical facilities. In this task they were assisted by the United States Aid Mission which set up a programme of its own.

In 1961-1962 the International Red Cross and the Swiss Association for Technical Assistance (SATA) established four permanent settlements in Nepal — at Jawalakhel in Kathmandu, Hyangja at Pokhara, Dhorpatan in the western mountains, and Chialsa in Solu — where the scattered refugees were concentrated and provided with basic necessities as well as education and instruction in handicrafts. As soon as the refugees were settled, efforts were made to find work for them. Carpet making was the favourite occupation and these organizations trained refugees to act as managers and accountants, and in this way made them independent.

Many of the refugees moved to India, where they were settled in camps and villages. About fourteen thousand remained in Nepal, five thousand of whom were still divided among twelve refugee camps in 1985 — Jawalakhel, Bodhnath, Swayambu, Pokhara, Tserok near Jomosom, Dhorpatan, Chialsa in Solu, Walong-chung in east Nepal and Rasua in the west. The camps were managed by staff members of the aid organizations (the Red Cross, Swiss Aid, etc.) but suitable refugees were trained to take over.

A carpet workshop and a day school for Tibetan children would be found in each of these camps. The children were taught Tibetan as well as Nepali reading, writing and history in the school, but the teaching of Tibetan history, culture and religion had priority. Parents were not encouraged to send their children to other schools where they might be alienated from Tibetan culture. The fees charged by the Tibetan schools are thirty rupees per month, but if parents are too poor to pay such fees, wealthier members of the community sponsor their children. Within the Tibetan community there is altogether a great deal of mutual help.

In every camp there is also a cooperative society with a shop selling goods at market rates. Such shops are managed by representatives of the communities. These representatives also settle disputes between Tibetans — Tibetans hardly ever appeal to regular Nepalese courts for adjudication of disputes within the community. The manager of a cooperative society does not draw a salary, but works on a voluntary basis.

Some Tibetans with Chinese passports occasionally cross the border to visit relatives living in Nepal. They usually return to Tibet athough some such visitors are persuaded to remain in Nepal.

Very few Tibetans settled in Nepal show an inclination to return to Tibet for good although some go there to visit family members who still live in Tibet. Usually they return to Nepal after some weeks, and say that they now have a much better life in Nepal than they would have if they decided to stay in Tibet permanently under present conditions.

6

Dharamsala

THE MAJOR FOCUS of Tibetan refugee's religious and national sentiments is Dharamsala, the present residence of His Holiness the Dalai Lama and the seat of many institutions serving the interest and cohesion of the thousands of Tibetans dispersed over the Indian subcontinent. While Lhasa is a nostalgic memory for the older generation and a vague dream for those who left Tibet as children, Dharamsala is a concrete centre of pilgrimage within reach of most Tibetans living in India and Nepal.

A generous and farsighted decision of the Government of India allowed the Dalai Lama and his entourage to take possession of this hill-station of British days, and to create a small township of distinctly Tibetan character. Located in northern India, the cool climate and background of towering mountains often covered in snow serve to make the Tibetans feel at home, and the large number of monks and Tibetans in traditional attire create an atmosphere which gives foreign tourists the impression of being on the threshold of the Tibetan cultural sphere.

About seven thousand Tibetans live more or less permanently in Dharamsala. To them it has replaced Lhasa as the 'Holy City' for wherever the Dalai Lama resides, in their view, is the seat of Tibet's government even if it is in exile. Incidentally the region has an aura of sanctity also in Tibetan literature for it figures in the lineage of the teachers of the Tibetan saint and poet Milarepa.

The majority of Tibetans stay in a crowded settlement known, since British time, as McLeod Ganj. The religious centre is the Tsuglagkhang, the cathedral designed as a replica of the Central Cathedral of Lhasa of the same name. A spacious and elegant building situated opposite the residence of the Dalai Lama, the Tsuglagkhang houses large images of the Buddha, Padmasambhava and Avalokiteshvara (the bodhisattva or saint of compassion, also called Chenresig) made of gilded bronze. The Avalokiteshvara image had been made for the Central Cathedral of Lhasa, but at the time of the Cultural

McLeod Ganj, near Dharamsala, India

Marketplace in McLeod Ganj

Revolution Red Guards dragged it out and left it lying in a street. Pious Tibetans managed to smuggle it via Nepal to Dharamsala where it was incorporated into a newly sculptured image and ultimately erected in the Central Cathedral. The new image, which was consecrated in 1970, is made of silver and has eleven faces and a thousand hands and eyes. The cathedral's large collection of books includes entire sets of *Kagyur* (teachings attributed to the historical Buddha) and *Tengyur* (discourses on the *Kagyur*), some three hundred and twenty-five volumes in all.

Most days the cathedral is crowded with monks and laymen assembled for prayers and the performance of rituals. If there is not room on the floor of the main hall, devotees sit on the verandah surrounding the core of the building and watch the services through open doors and windows. The Dalai Lama frequently walks from his residence to the cathedral and leads the prayers.

Close to the cathedral and the residence of the Dalai Lama is the Namgyal Monastery, an institution founded in the sixteenth century in Lhasa by the third Dalai Lama and characterized by its catholicity, which allows prayers and rites of all Tibetan sects to take place within its walls. This monastery, whose monks used to be housed in the Potala palace but were driven out by the Chinese, was also recreated in Dharamsala.

Not far from the cathedral and Namgyal monastery stands a nunnery

The Dalai Lama leading services at the Tsuglagkhang Central Cathedral in Dharamsala, with statue of Avalokiteshvara (Chenresig) in background

known as Ganden Choling, founded in 1972 by two Tibetan nuns, Ngawang Chozin and Ngawang Peldon. The initial twelve nuns have grown in number to seventy, and the nuns are now well known and highly respected. Tibetan girls from many settlements in India have joined the nunnery, and donations offered by Tibetans with requests for the performance of special prayer rites help to support the nuns.

The Buddhist School of Dialectics was opened in Dharamsala in 1973 and attracts monks from all Buddhist sects. Mongolians, Indians and numerous Buddhists from Western countries are among the student body. In addition to a general course on Buddhist philosophy, the school offers a seven-year course on *Prajna-paramita* (The Six Perfections) and a three year course on the Indian Buddhist philosopher Nagarjuna's *Treatise on the Middle Way.* The presence of students from the United States, Britain, Germany, France, other European and Western countries lends Dharamsala an international character unusual among religious institutions in India.

Different in many ways is the Tushita Retreat Centre — founded in 1972 by Lama Thubten Yeshi — located in the hills above McLeod Ganj amidst caves occupied for many years by Tibetan lamas and yogis who found the seclusion and peaceful atmosphere which they needed for meditation and general spiritual exercises in such hermitages.

In and around Dharamsala various institutions have been created with the

Tibetan Institute of Performing Arts ensemble in Dharamsala

Tibetan Institute of Performing Arts (TIPA) performance in traditional costume

Tibetan woman spinning wool in McLeod Ganj area of Dharamsala

express purpose of assisting the preservation and revival of Tibetan culture. The Tibetan Institute of Performing Arts (TIPA) is the home of actors, dancers and singers engaged in mounting theatrical performances in traditional style. TIPA maintains its own costume tailoring shop, mask-making workshop and instrument making section, and there are trained instructors who regularly visit Tibetan schools outside Dharamsala to spread the knowledge of theatrical arts. On national holidays and other propitious occasions, members of TIPA perform dances and contemporary plays. Folk operas, dance programmes and concerts are staged in suitable places every April. The institute also presents Tibetan theatrical art to audiences in India and Nepal and occasionally even in Western countries.

Wherever Tibetan refugees have settled, handicrafts and particularly weaving and carpet making are foremost among the activities serving their maintenance, and in Dharamsala too a major centre is devoted to the production of carpets, textiles and Tibetan woolen wearing apparel.

Gangchen Kyishong

What is popularly referred to as Dharamsala is not a compact conurbation but a hilly area where clusters of buildings including the residence of the Dalai Lama and the Central Cathedral are scattered over a rugged and still partly wooded terrain. Within this, only two localities — McLeod Ganj and Gangchen Kyishong — have the appearance of a planned settlement, with

Gangchen Kyishong

McLeod Ganj having by far the larger population. Built on a steep hillside, Gangchen Kyishong, on the other hand, can boast the more remarkable buildings designed in Tibetan style with decorative bands of red and black framing the white-washed walls.

The cluster known as the Central Secretariat houses all departments of the Administration-in-Exile. Close by is the office of the Assembly of Tibetan People's Deputies, which functions as the parliament of the Tibetan population in exile. The most impressive and lavishly decorated building in the cluster, the Library of Tibetan Works and Archives contains a large collection of Tibetan printed works and manuscripts, as well as books in Western languages relating to Tibet and other Buddhist countries. Generally referred to as 'the Library,' this building also serves as a museum containing ancient valuable objects and pictures. Moreover, teams of Tibetan scholars engaged in research, translation and documentation have their offices and lecture rooms in this building. Research students from many countries work there too, and occasionally religious rituals performed and attended by such students take place in some of the large halls of the library building. The staff is engaged also in the publication of Tibetan scholarly books and a periodical published in English under the title *Tibet Journal.* Printing presses located in Gangchen Kyishong have produced many Tibetan language publications including textbooks for Tibetan schools in India and Nepal. The Library has the reputation of being a centre of Tibetan studies accessible to and frequented by numerous foreign students. According to statistics compiled by the staff, more than a thousand scholars from over twenty countries have pursued studies in Tibetan language and philosophy there.

From the Library it is only a few steps to the magnificent Nechung Monastery, which is the seat of the Nechung Oracle, one of the most important state oracles of Tibet and traditionally closely associated with the Dalai Lama. This Oracle's secret rituals are believed to go back to the eighth century and to the great Guru Rinpoche (Padmasambhava). The Nechung gonpa is one of the finest buildings, lavishly decorated outside as well as in the large hall where the Oracle is supposed to fall into a trance and pronounce his prophesies which have played a role in the search for the new incarnation of a Dalai Lama in the past.

The Nechung Oracle is the most important but not the only state oracle in the area of Dharamsala. The Gardhong State Oracle is also in Gangchen Kyishong, with a gonpa of its own that is well furnished and decorated though not as grand as the Nechung Gonpa. The medium through whose mouth the prophecies are communicated was, in 1985, still a young man who lived in a house close to the Gardhong Gonpa. He stated that he was too young and inexperienced to act as oracle for important official decisions, and therefore he kept in the background.

Efforts to prevent a decline of traditional skills in the visual arts include the maintenance and funding of a small school of thanka painting where young monks are being trained as painters by an old and knowledgeable Tibetan thanka painter. There is also a parallel small school of wood carvers and thus the visual aspects of Tibetan cultural life are being carefully nurtured. Considering the narrow economic basis of Tibetan communities in exile, the determination to keep alive even non-profit cultural activities is all the more admirable. Yet it is consistent with the general policy to preserve not only Buddhist religion but also most aspects of traditional Tibetan culture.

This purpose is served too by the publication of a considerable number of journals and magazines in Tibetan and English. The Information Office publishes a monthly news magazine called *Sheja* (Knowledge) which is read by most literate Tibetans. Another periodical in Tibetan called *Lhaksam Tsekpa*, published by the Institute of Buddhist Dialectics, is meant to interpret Western ideas and political trends to literate Tibetans. Publications in English introduce Westerners to the Buddhist spiritual world as well as the present social and political problems of refugees engaged in rebuilding Tibetan culture outside Tibet.

Many children were separated from their parents during the exodus from Tibet, or became orphaned altogether because their fathers were killed in encounters with pursuing Chinese soldiers and their mothers did not survive the hardship of the trek across snow covered Himalayan passes. Arrangements were made in Dharamsala as well as some settlements in south India for children who could not find protection and maintenance in the families of relatives. The largest and best organized of these orphanages is the Tibetan Children's Village situated on the top of a hill-range some nine kilometers from the main part of Dharamsala. Hostels, individual houses, school buildings, staff quarters and handicraft training centres have been erected, and a dedicated staff occasionally augmented by foreign volunteers has been

Above and Opposite: Tibetan Children's Village in Dharamsala

looking after children of all ages ever since the foundation of the village in 1960. The Tibetan Children's Village also served as a model for similar institutions in south India and Ladakh. It is estimated that some five thousand children have passed through the village at Dharamsala, some of whom later joined more advanced boarding schools and colleges in various parts of India.

The great attraction of Dharamsala is not only the personality of the Dalai Lama — revered as of old by the Tibetan people notwithstanding the continuous Chinese attempts to undermine his authority and prestige — but also the presence of numerous Buddhist devotees from many countries of East and West who assemble there for the purpose of acquiring knowledge of Buddhist doctrine and Tibetan culture. In addition to Indians, Nepalis, Burmese and Asians from other regions, young men and women of many Western countries come to Dharamsala to study and meditate. Their active participation in rituals and prayer sessions is undoubtedly an inspiration for young Tibetans to concentrate on the study of scriptures and on research about the nature and history of their own religion. The worldwide admiration for Buddhist religion and practice stands in striking contrast to the contempt expressed by the Chinese rulers.

In addition to the Tsuglagkhang and the Namgyal Monastery attached to the cathedral, there are several minor monasteries and other religious centres in the area of Dharamsala. The great Tibetan monastery of Ganden — whose monks established their main centre in exile in south India — maintains two

Kyabje Ling Dorje Chang, the late Senior Tutor to the Dalai Lama, leading a long-life prayer ceremony at the Central Cathedral in Dharamsala

branch colleges, called Shartse and Jangtse, in McLeod Ganj. Branches of the Gyuto and Gyume Tantric Colleges are also located in McLeod Ganj. Two high ranking lamas have their residences in Dharamsala: Ling Labrang, the residence of Kyabje Ling Dorje Chang, the late Senior Tutor to the Dalai Lama, and Trichang Labrang, the residence of Kyabje Trichang Dorje, the Junior Tutor. Their prestige as eminent scholars has made them focal points of interest for visiting lamas and devotees.

Centres for specific ritual performances are the Nyungne Lhakang and the Lhagyal-ri. The former has the responsibility of organizing the *nyungne,* a ritual connected with an annual period of fasting, and the latter is a place where Tibetans perform propitiation rites for the protecting deities and guardian gods.

In view of the importance and large number of religious institutions in Dharamsala one may wonder why no large monasteries — such as the new foundations at Bodhnath in Kathmandu — have been established at the very centre of Tibetan Buddhist life in India. The reason for this apparent neglect of an opportunity is perhaps the lack of a large population whose efforts and financial resources can support relatively large monastic communities. Dharamsala has a population of only fifteen thousand, not all of it Tibetan or in economic circumstances capable of funding the construction of large monastery buildings and maintaining hundreds of monks such as those supported

The Dalai Lama greets a pilgrim from Tibet

by the substantial population of Kathmandu and the many Buddhists of various origin settled in the Nepal Valley.

Dharamsala is sometimes referred to as 'A Little Lhasa' even in official publications, yet there are considerable differences in the structure of traditional Tibetan society and the social pattern of Tibetan communities in exile. This becomes apparent even at the apex of Dharamsala society.

The Dalai Lama is no longer a figure radiating an aura of mystery who lives in complete isolation, accessible only to a small circle of clerics and officials of the highest status, as he and his predecessors did in Lhasa. He appears often in public, participating in services in the Central Cathedral, and spends much of his time granting audiences to a variety of visitors to Dharamsala. Having traveled widely in both Eastern and Western countries, the Dalai Lama is now open to contacts with foreigners of all nationalities. His fluency in English enables him to converse freely with visitors and to lecture to academic audiences in the United States and other English speaking countries. The purpose of such travels is mainly to arouse sympathy with the cause of the Tibetans in exile and also to spread interest in Buddhism.

There is a certain similarity between the lifestyle of the present Pope and that of the Dalai Lama. Each is the head of one of the world's largest religious communities, and each is universally accorded the title 'His Holiness.' Both have moved out of the restricted atmosphere of highly selective circles and deliberately travel through the wide world, not shunning contact with large numbers of their devotees. Incidentally there is yet another parallel between these two highly revered religious heads for both are at the forefront of the battle of spiritual faith against the forces of Marxist materialism.

Not only the Dalai Lama has changed his social style by freely mixing with people of all classes and backgrounds, but the many reincarnate lamas now staying in Dharamsala and other Tibetan centres in India and Nepal no longer distance themselves from the ordinary laymen as they tended to do as long as they held the exalted position of abbots in their own monasteries. While every tulku is still regarded with respect, the awe a reincarnated head of a monastery inspired among layfolk has now largely diminished. A one-time abbot, though still enjoying the prestige of a reincarnation, cannot retain the authority he wielded as long as he was in command of a large community of monks.

A similar change in status has affected members of the former aristocracy. Among the refugees now living in India and Nepal are several Tibetans of noble origin including descendants of the rulers of small Tibetan states known as *gyal-rig*. Although they are still accorded respect, it is comparable that enjoyed by the French nobility after the revolution of the 1770s. A few were accommodated in the Dalai Lama's administration but others are without power and have no special privileges. The same fate has befallen aristocrats known as ku-dr'ag who used to have access to high office in the government of independent Tibet.

In the feudal order of Tibet before the Chinese invasion, marriages between members of different social classes were unusual. As class-consciousness is one of the features of Tibetan societies which has survived defeat and exile, nobles still prefer to marry their social equals. Class barriers are gradually being lowered, however, particularly among the younger generation educated in Indian universities. Academic status and success in professional activities have become criteria to be considered in the choice of marriage partners. This development is largely due to the effect of the educational programme sponsored by the Dalai Lama's administration. By 1984, some five hundred Tibetans were studying at various universities and there were four hundred and forty-seven graduate and postgraduate teachers, most of whom were employed in Tibetan schools. There are also numerous young Tibetans who have obtained professional jobs, having qualified in such fields as medicine or engineering.

The growth of monastic institutions in the Kathmandu Valley suggests, however, that although many educational avenues are open to young Tibetans a religious career still has considerable attraction. Even in the settlements in south India, which are far removed from the Buddhist atmosphere pervading parts of Nepal, there seems to be no shortage of recruits to the monasteries established by lamas from such Tibetan gonpa as Sera, Ganden and Drepung.

Wandering story-telling monk in Dharamsala

Buddhist monk at Sera monastery in Mundgod in south India

7

Tibetans in South India

SOME TIBETAN REFUGEES were able to settle in Nepal among populations sharing a common cultural background and, most importantly, the value system of Mahayana Buddhism. In regions of eastern Nepal such as Solu and Khumbu they found acceptance by local Sherpa inhabitants who welcomed lamas from Tibet as a useful addition to the somewhat depleted ranks of the Sherpa clergy. Whole monastic communities — who escaped across the Tibet-Nepal frontier before the arrival of Chinese forces — established themselves on Nepalese soil and within a short time built monasteries in the style of those they had left beyond the Himalayas.

Tibetan emigrants also felt at home and mingled easily with local populations in western Nepal. Places such as Lo-Manthang (Mustang) were virtually Tibetan towns and the ruler — referred to as Lo Gyalpo or Mustang Raja — was in fact a Tibetan prince with family connections in Lhasa. Culturally, Nepalese borderlands were an ideal refuge, but their economic resources were far too limited to permit the permanent settlement of thousands or even hundreds of Tibetans.

Most Tibetan refugees had no choice but to move south to seek asylum and ultimately a home in India. Fortunately for the Tibetans, newly independent India was not in sympathy with China and made every effort to accommodate as many Tibetans as possible. Dependence on Indian aid and hospitality had begun at the top of the Tibetan hierarchic structure, and the Dalai Lama and many high ranking members of his government had been helped to settle at Dharamsala and its vicinity. Substantial numbers of Tibetan refugees were accommodated in other parts of India at the same time. The Government of India established large Tibetan settlements in Orissa and Arunachal Pradesh, providing them with considerable acreages of cultivable land. The Indian policy was to resettle Tibetans in groups of several thousands to enable them to retain their language, culture and social institutions. Settlers were also permitted a high degree of administrative autonomy under the overall control of the Dalai Lama's government in Dharamsala. The largest rehabilitation project was located in the erstwhile Mysore State where extensive stretches of forest land were made available for clearance and subsequent cultivation by Tibetans.

The first settlements to be founded under this project were established near a place referred to by the pseudonym Mundakuppa, which is situated between the cities of Mysore and Arracrem. It lies at an elevation of about twenty-seven hundred feet and has an average rainfall of thirty-five inches. Although neither the climate nor the environment resemble the Tibetans' homeland, the new settlers succeeded in developing a self-reliant farming economy within a short time. The oldest Tibetan settlement in Karnataka is Mundugot (or Mundgod) in north Kanara District, with about twenty-six hundred inhabitants. Gurupura, in Mysore District, houses twenty-six hundred inhabitants including two hundred and fifty lamas; Byllakuppe in Coorg District has a population of twelve thousand, many of whom came from Sera Gonpa in Tibet; Bailu in Mysore District has about twenty-six hundred inhabitants, and the smallest settlement Tshokura on the borders of Mysore and Coorg has only two hundred and fifty residents.

All the settlers are devout Buddhists but not all adhere to the same sect. Thus in Byllakuppe there are gonpa of several sects — Gelukpa, Nyingma-pa, Sakyapa and Kagyupa — and among the lamas attached to these gonpa there are several reincarnations (tulku).

Each village elects a leader for a period of about three years. He is responsible for the maintenance of order within the settlement and acts as spokesman for the villagers in dealings with the Indian population in the surrounding area. A Tibetan Cooperative Society with a secretary who is paid by the Dalai Lama's office in Dharamsala provides an institutionalized link with the Dalai Lama. This society coordinates the major economic activities of all settlements in Karnataka, provides them with tractors and other agricultural machinery, and assists the farmers with marketing of crops. The Government of India's overall supervision of the entire scheme of settling the refugees lies in the hands of the Tibetan Rehabilitation Office headed by an Assistant Commissioner.

Tibetan Settlements in Gurupura

When I visited Gurupura in February 1985 I was impressed by the high standard of living attained by the Tibetans. The state government allocated some four thousand acres of cultivable land to the community, given on a lease of ninety-nine years and not as an outright grant. Since Tibetans are regarded as 'guests' and not Indian citizens, they cannot be given land on permanent tenure. The policy of the Tibetans is not to accept Indian citizenship because they still hope to return to Tibet and want to retain their status as nationals of an independent Tibet. The ambiguous nature of their present right to land at Gurupura has not deflected them from developing their holdings to the best of their ability. Though not all of them had an agricultural background when they arrived from Tibet, they have proved efficient farmers growing crops of sorghum, maize, finger millet *(Eleusine coracana),* pulses and various vegetables. They use well irrigation wherever possible but the cultivation of rice is not practicable except in a few places. Most households have acquired cattle, both as dairy animals and for use as plow bullocks. Goats and sheep are kept to provide meat, which has always been an important item in the Tibetan diet but is too expensive in Karnataka to be purchased regularly in the market. On the whole the Tibetan settlers have adjusted well to the general life-style which they had to adopt in south India. They have built good houses incorporating some Tibetan features such as painting the outer walls in white and red. Flat roofs typical of Tibet are not suitable for the climate of south India, so slanting roofs covered with tiles are used to protect houses against the heavy rains of the monsoon season. Most houses stand in clusters but each has a small garden with trees and flowering shrubs. Prayer flags are raised on the roofs or on tall masts standing in the gardens.

One Gurupura settlement accommodates the two hundred and fifty lamas living in the colony, and a spacious gonpa had been built in this settlement. Six steps lead up to a covered porch protected by a tiled roof, and from this porch one gains access to the main building which is square and contains the large dukhang. The outside walls are painted white and on the front facade they support a false extension consisting of a free standing wall about four feet high and painted with black and white decorations in the shape of small circles. In the centre of the roof of the gonpa are two gilded spires and one gilded wheel *(chakra).* The interior of the building is almost completely dedicated to the dukhang, which is a rather bare hall with a simple altar bearing a few statues and a minimum of ritual objects. A few thanka hang on the walls but there are no frescoes such as are usual in gonpa in Tibet and the Himalayan regions of Nepal, Sikkim and Bhutan.

The community of lamas is structured on traditional lines, with gonpa officials such as *umze, nyerwa* and *chorpon* attending to the rituals. All lamas and novices wear the usual wine-red Tibetan garments, even though they must be uncomfortable in the heat of the south Indian summer.

One house in the lama settlement of Gurupura is set aside for prominent guests, and I was told that the Dalai Lama had stayed there during one of his visits to the Tibetan colonies in Karnataka.

In the same settlement there is also a large workshop where carpets are manufactured for sale in India as well as for export. Seventy-five Tibetans, drawn from among all the households of Gurupura, are employed in this workshop. The wool is obtained from Ladakh and Australia, as south Indian sheep wool is not suitable for carpet making or even for weaving textiles for clothing. While lamas wear exclusively their traditional red garments, lay-men tend to compromise in the matter of dress and normally wear the lighter Indian or Western-type clothes, though most preserve some Tibetan outfits for ceremonial occasions. Women are more intent on retaining their Tibetan identity and hence have not taken to the wearing of the traditional Indian women's *sari* but stick to the wearing of traditional Tibetan clothes.

The Tibetans' skill in weaving woolen cloth and carpets has given them an advantage not possessed by other refugee communities settled in India, such as Hindus who fled from Bangladesh. Tibetan carpets are a commodity much in demand in some of the most affluent countries of the West, and carpets are not perishable and can be easily transported. Moreover, Tibetans have always been skillful traders and organizers, and are hence in a favour-able position to market the products of artisans employed in the workshops. Carpet making has also the advantage that men, women and children can be used in certain stages of the production. Altogether there are nine Tibetan carpet workshops in Karnataka.

Cash earnings from the manufacture of carpets have benefited also the Tibetans' farming activities, enabling them to purchase agricultural mach-inery and to employ Indians as wage-labourers. The resilience and spirit of enterprise so typical of Tibetans could not be better demonstrated than by the fact that soon after arriving in a strange country as penniless refugees they managed to recruit local low-caste Hindus as farm labourers, paying their wages out of earnings from trade and in some cases carpet making. As their agricultural economy expanded, they gradually became entrepreneurs similar to Indian high-caste landlords depending on the labour of Harijans. This cooperation with the lowest classes in the local society had the advan-tage also of acquiring workers familiar with agricultural techniques appro-priate to the climatic and ecological conditions of south India.

The tactful conduct of the Tibetan newcomers is attested by the fact that their economic success, and particularly their incursions into the local labour pool, did not antagonize the upper strata of the indigenous Hindu population. There seems to have been little friction between the local farmers and the Tibetan settlers. To forestall any resentment of old established land-owners against strangers from a distant land, the Government of India had made it clear to the local people that the settlement of Tibetans was a temporary measure, and ultimately they would return to their homeland. It was not envisaged that a solution to the problem might not occur for a very long time, but even though repatriation of the refugees in the foreseeable future appears now highly unlikely, relations between Tibetans and the local population of Karnataka have remained amicable and there is no public demand for their departure. The Tibetans have been careful not to encroach on any right or interest of their Hindu neighbours and the latter have learnt to respect the religious institutions and practices of the newcomers, whose ideology and rituals conform to their own beliefs and customs in many ways.

Apart from these ideological factors favouring good relations between Tibetans and Indians, material developments also helped to establish amicable cooperation between the two ethnic groups. The Representative of the Dalai Lama did his best to ensure that the presence of Tibetans and their growing prosperity also benefited local Indians. Tractors and trucks bought for the Tibetans were made available for Indian landowners to hire whenever they could be spared. Similarly, poor landless Indians profited from the Tibetans' need for casual agricultural labourers. Shopkeepers and traders in nearby villages and towns derived some benefits from economic development of the region, due in part at least to financial aid provided to Tibetans by the Government of India as well as international charitable agencies channeled to Karnataka by the Dalai Lama's organization.

Tibetan Settlements in Byllakuppe

Gurupura is one of the smaller Tibetan settlements in south India. At no great distance from Hunsur lies the far larger and more important settlement of Byllakuppe, which I had the opportunity to visit in January 1986. Arriving there by the main road from Mysore, I realized at once that this was a place of a quite different nature. Several hamlets inhabited by about twelve thousand Tibetans are dispersed over a large area, and each has a monastery as its focal point.

Sera Monastery in Byllakuppe in south India

These monasteries serve the religious needs of Gelukpa, Nyingmapa and Kagyupa communities. In 1959 the first of these monasteries was founded by some three hundred monks of the great Sera monastery in Tibet. The original monastery of Sera consisted of the two gonpa of the Sera Jey College and the Sera Me College, and this division was perpetuated in its 'colony' in Karnataka. Each section has a great prayer hall (dukhang) of its own. In addition, an equally big hall known as Lachi Gonpa serves for ritual performances attended by monks of both sections of Sera. Each of the two sections is headed by a *khanpo* (abbot or administrator), a position held by one of the senior exiles from Sera in Tibet. The khanpo of Sera Jey College is known as Lobsang Tange, and the khanpo of Sera Me College as Themba Pondzo.

Buildings containing the two sections of Sera are constructed in Tibetan style and appointed in red and white. Limitations of space, material and cost did not permit the construction of even a miniature replica of the enormous Tibetan Sera monastery, but sufficient traditional features have been incorporated in the design to give the monks the impression of being in a Tibetan environment. The three great prayer halls are richly decorated and furnished with precious brocade hangings on all the pillars and some of the walls. Wooden parts of the structure are elaborately painted in red, green, yellow and other bright colours. Although the monks had not been able to carry more than a few precious objects and books on their flight from Tibet, artists among

Ganden Monastery in Mundgod, south India

the exiles recreated many of the statues and paintings which had to be left behind in Sera where they were subsequently destroyed by fanatical Chinese. Large statues of Tsongkhapa, Phagpa Chenresig (Tibetan name for the Budd ia of Compassion), other saints and divinities stand on the altar in each prayer hall, with various ritual objects among them. Long rows of cushions, on which the monks sit during services, cover the greater part of the floor of the hall.

I arrived in Byllakuppe on the day before the Tibetan New Year celebration. Bread, sweetmeats and fruits were heaped in each gonpa hall, along with collections of various bottles containing drinks to be consumed by monks and worshipers. Streets were alive with monks in red garments engaged in various activities connected with preparations for the New Year celebrations.

While many inhabitants of Byllakuppe spend much of their time on ritual practices, it is obvious that the two hundred acres of cultivable land allotted to the Tibetans are being carefully tilled. The main crops are maize and millet, but where sources of irrigation are available there is also cultivation of rice which the Tibetans have learnt from their Indian neighbours. Bullocks are used for plowing, but some tractors have been recently acquired and are used in rotation by members of the village community.

All dwelling houses in Gurupura are built in Tibetan style with flat roofs. In Byllakuppe, only monastery buildings have flat roofs, and the houses of lay people are built in local style with gabled roofs covered by red bricks. I was told that this was done for reasons of economy, because tiled roofs are much cheaper to construct than flat roofs made rain-proof by layers of cement. Because of the adoption of the local Indian style of architecture, Byllakuppe lacks the typical Tibetan character which is so striking in Gurupura.

The many monks wearing red robes, however, lend Byllakuppe a Tibetan appearance and, while men among the lay-folk do not wear Tibetan dress, the women retain their traditional Tibetan type of clothes as much as possible, even though they have to compromise in the sort of textiles used.

The outward appearance of Byllakuppe, apart from the monasteries, is Indian rather than Tibetan but the life-style of the inhabitants follows traditional Tibetan patterns. There are numerous tulku, some adults and others adolescents. Several of these reincarnations were born in Tibet and came to Byllakuppe after the Chinese invasion of Tibet, but some younger tulku were born in India and now reside at the Sera Gonpa where they study under the guidance of senior monks.

Tibetan Settlements at Mundgod and other Indian locations

Monasteries were also founded in the northern part of Karnataka by exiled monks of some of the great Tibetan gonpa. The establishment of the 'colonies' of the Ganden and Drepung monasteries in Tibet began in 1960, sharing a site known as Mundgod, near the Indian towns of Dharwar and Hubli. These gonpa are situated about three to four kilometers from each other. Each is divided into two sections, and in addition there are also settlements of Sakya and Nyingmapa communities. The number of Tibetans at Mundgod is approximately six thousand. As in Byllakuppe there are several buildings serving as accommodation for the monks and novices, and in the centre of each section lies a great prayer-hall (dukhang) sumptuously fitted out with statues and ritual requisites and decorated with silk hangings and paintings in bright colours.

Monks are engaged in upkeep of the buildings and also work in printing workshops and the libraries. While in Tibet there was no need for monks to engage in farmwork, the taboo on manual work has been waved in Karnataka and monks regularly join the laymen in some agricultural activities.

Another Tibetan settlement in Karnataka was established at the Cauvery Valley, fifty-four miles east of the city of Mysore. This has been named Dekyi Larsoe and was occupied by about two thousand refugees who arrived from 1969 to 1978 after leaving temporary camps at Simla, Kulu, Dharamsala and Gangtok.

In addition to the settlements in Karnataka, there are numerous camps and villages of Tibetan refugees in other parts of India. Among these, the following deserve to be listed:

Norgyeling in Bandara District of Maharashtra lies some sixty kilometers west of Nagpur. It was opened in 1972 to accommodate over eight hundred refugees who came from Dalhousie, Dharamsala, Kulu, Darjeeling and Orissa, who were joined by refugees from two other places in India.

Fendeyling is an agricultural settlement at Mainpat in Madhya Pradesh. It was opened in 1963 when two thousand and eighty Tibetans arrived from road camps in Kulu and Kangra, but could not be all absorbed.

Dhargyeling, situated in the Lohit valley near Tezu in Arunachal Pradesh, was established in 1962 for a population of about twelve thousand people. The settlers came between 1962 and 1968 from different parts of Tibet and had crossed the Indian border at various places. They had to clear dense forest before they could start cultivation.

Choephelling lies at Miao in Tirap District of Arunachal Pradesh. The settlers had previously stayed at Changdang in Tirap District and moved to Cheophelling in 1976.

Tenzingang lies in Kameng District in Arunachal Pradesh northeast of Bomdila. Some of the settlers had previously stayed at Dalhousie and others at Pithoragarh in Uttar Pradesh.

Churning butter for a Tibetan wedding in Rajpur, India

Monk with hand printing press at Swayambunath monastery

8

The Lifestyle of Monks

DURING THE EARLY part of the Middle Ages, the cultural traditions of the Western world were preserved largely by Christian monks who carefully copied and edited much of the literature of classical Greece and Rome. Similarly, the literature — and indeed most of the cultural traditions of Tibet — are being preserved by Buddhist monks who have saved large parts of the Tibetan sacred scriptures from the holocaust of organized destruction of Tibetan culture and religion by the Chinese military and vandals let loose during the so-called Cultural Revolution.

With most Tibetan monasteries in ruins and the contents of many of their libraries used as firewood by the Chinese, there would be little chance of reconstructing Tibetan religious scriptures from the fragments hidden on Tibetan soil were it not for the courageous efforts of monks who carried yak-loads of sacred books across Himalayan passes to safety in Nepal and India. Whole communities of Buddhist monks are dedicating their lives to the task of preserving the Tibetan lifestyle in the countries of their adoption, wherever they have been able to settle.

In a few cases, entire monastic communities were able to move *en masse* into neighbouring countries without the dispersal of monks, and in such circumstances it was possible to establish monasteries with the same human resources which had been concentrated in parent institutions in Tibet. Such is the case with Thupten Choling, the recently founded monastery close to Junbesi in the Sherpa region of Solu in Nepal, whose inhabitants moved there in a body under their own abbot when they had to flee their parent monastery of Rongbo, as we saw earlier. This wholesale transfer of a community was possible because of the proximity of Rongbo to the Nepalese border and availability of a suitable site among a Buddhist population with long-standing connections with Rongbo.

Most Tibetan monasteries in Nepal and India have a different history. Most owe their existence to the arrival of a reincarnate lama accompanied by a small number of monks who joined him on the flight from Tibet and shared in his endeavour to establish a new monastery outside Tibet. Several monasteries at Bodhnath and Swayambunath came into being in this way rather than by the migration of an entire monastic community (see Chapters 11 and 12). While at the beginning there may have been no more than eight or ten monks, their numbers increased as refugee lamas joined the founding fathers and new novices were recruited, mainly from Tibetan families settled in the Nepal Valley. But not only Tibetans were eligible for entry into an incipient monastic community. Young people of such local Buddhist populations as Sherpas, Tamangs, Newars, Manangis and other Bhotia groups sought admission to new monasteries headed by prestigious reincarnate lamas.

In such heterogeneous communities there is obviously a need for strict discipline and this is administered according to traditional rules as they prevailed in most Tibetan monasteries. The majority of monks were selected for a religious life by their parents and sent to a monastery for education and study at an early age before they could have expressed any preference of their own. They were expected initially to learn to read and write, without having to commit themselves to an ascetic life involving abstention from certain worldly occupations. Only at a later stage, after they have learnt to read Tibetan, would they take a vow known as *rabdzung,* which commits them to a life of celibacy and abstention from trading and the cultivation of land.

The abstinence of a monk from such activities involves the need to draw

Kim Yeshi

Buddhist monks engaged in debate

upon donations from laymen for his subsistence. In Tibet the monks' maintenance was largely met from economic resources owned by their monasteries, such as land and livestock, but monasteries in Nepal and most parts of India do not possess such capital. There, monks have to be maintained by contributions from their own families and by fees received in payment for religious services which they render to laymen.

In all these arrangements, a certain basic conflict springs from the fact that ideally monks should renounce the material world but in practice they rely on the support of laymen for their subsistence and this depends inevitably on the latter's success in the handling of material matters. Transactions between laymen and monks are not of the same nature as one-sided gifts to charities, however. While a layman's contributions provide a monk's means of sub- sistence, the monk — by accepting the gifts — confers merit on the layman who had given them.

There is a considerable difference between the economic base of a small community of monks in a monastery supported by the lay-folk of one or two nearby villages which have traditional ties to that monastery, and the eco- nomic position of newly founded monasteries of Tibetan refugees whose traditional supporters had died at the hands of the Chinese, remained in their Tibetan home villages, or dispersed over numerous settlements in Nepal or India. In the latter case, the monks have no certain and continuing source of income. Rather, they must rely upon the casual generosity of devotees and upon their own earnings from ritual services rendered to visitors or to families living in the vicinity who are inclined to commission one or several monks to perform such rituals as they consider beneficial to their well-being now or in the world beyond.

In my study of the Sherpa village of Khumjung, I recorded the ritual activities of a single lama residing in that village over a four month period. This lama, who was originally from Kham in eastern Tibet, spent one hundred and four days during that period in performing rituals for which he had been commissioned. The large number of engagements was due to the long-standing relationship he had built up with many of the villagers. A monk in one of the new Tibetan monasteries in Kathmandu has little chance of collecting a comparable number of engagements, because he depends on casual invitations and is unlikely to already have a permanent clientele.

Although most monasteries of Sherpas and other Bhotias in Nepal had been modeled on the pattern of Tibetan monasteries, they were of much smaller size than even medium sized monastic establishments in Tibet. Large monasteries in Tibet — such as Sera, Drepung and Ganden — had hundreds and even thousands of monks in residence, but since the Chinese extended their anti-religious rule over Tibet such large monastic communities are no longer tolerated there. Newly established monasteries in Nepal and India are relatively small because there are not sufficient funds for the establishment and maintenance of enormous institutions.

Yet, whether large or small, Buddhist monasteries of all the four sects are organized according to a generally accepted tradition. Ideally, a monastery should be headed by a reincarnate lama (tulku), but a senior monk known as khanpo may act as abbot in the absence of such a reincarnation. In the huge Tibetan monasteries, a complex hierarchy of officials was necessary to organize the activities of hundreds of monks, but the rank order of monks is being maintained and the various offices are filled according to seniority even in small monasteries. Younger monks must pass through the lower ranks before becoming eligible for more responsible and prestigious posts, whose incumbents control both religious and material affairs of the monastery.

Monasteries in the Kathmandu Valley founded by refugee Tibetan monks inevitably differ from the monasteries in Tibet as well as from the older Sherpa monasteries established several generations ago. None of them have landholdings large enough to provide appreciable contributions to the monks' subsistence. Hence the monks have to exert themselves to find sources of income, and this means they must develop amicable relationships with affluent patrons. At Bodhnath the number of wealthy laymen of Buddhist persuasion is not large, but there are some traders and shopkeepers and every year new buildings are springing up, many of them built by Buddhists such as Sherpas and Manangis who decided to move into the proximity of the focal point of Buddhist revival. Such newcomers employ lamas for performance of domestic ceremonies and also commission larger rituals to be performed in the new gonpa.

Monks invited to visit the houses of such settlers for the recitation of prayers or funeral celebrations are entertained with choice food and drink as long as the ritual lasts, and are also paid an appropriate fee. Any cash they receive for their services should normally be passed on to their monastery, but it is said that some junior monks spend part of their fees on luxuries such as hiring taxis for the journey between the monastery and the client's house where the ritual takes place. Older people disapprove of this, but in view of the location of some of the new monasteries close to the modernized parts of Kathmandu and the resultant mingling of monks and Nepalese influenced by a Western lifestyle, the deviation of some monks from the traditional Tibetan way of life is not surprising. Indeed, the basic compliance of the majority of monks with a conduct first developed in the highly conservative atmosphere of Tibet is a remarkable social development

The tolerance with which abbots and other gonpa officials treat some youthful evasions of monastery rules can perhaps be explained by the great value placed on retaining novices and monks within the Tibetan monastic system. Only gross indiscipline or serious offenses against the rule of celibacy may occasionally lead to eviction of a monk from his monastery.

Celibacy

In most Tibetan monasteries, monks are required to lead a celibate life. Gelukpa monasteries place a strong emphasis on celibacy, whereas Nyingmapa and Kagyupa institutions are less strict and in Nepal there were some Nyingmapa gonpas — such as that of Thami in Khumbu — where most monks and even the abbot were married. In Tibet, monks had little opportunity to meet women for they spent most of their time among other monks and under the supervision of gonpa officials. Rarely mixing with lay people, there were few occasions when a young monk might be led astray, and a lama who offended against his vow of chastity was reproved, punished, fined and possibly ejected from the monastery.

In the Tibetan refugee communities, discipline is less rigid and particularly the monks who travel abroad have opportunities to meet women. In recent years some lamas, including some reincarnations, have married. Their marriages were met with an understanding attitude, although the traditional rules of their sects applied and the lamas could not continue to hold their previous posts in monasteries unless they belonged to a sect whose rules permitted marriage.

While in principle a monk renounces all worldly possessions at his ordination, some small concessions have to be made to enable him to live and operate in the material world. A monk may own and handle minor amounts of money and portable material goods, and may accept cash as fee for religious services and spend it for such purposes as hiring transport. The general modernization of life in the Kathmandu Valley as well as in south

Monks gather in Bodh Gaya, India for initiation ceremony

India makes such concessions inevitable, and it seems that monks are not troubled by their breaches of the rules of austerity because they know that otherwise it would be impossible to interact with laymen, whose support is essential for the maintenance of the monasteries.

Similar conflicts of principles arise in most Buddhist societies. Writing about Thai monks in her book *Buddhist Monk and Layman* (Cambridge, 1973), Jane Bunnag has emphasized that the ascetic regime of the monk — though intended to remove him from lay society — renders him dependent on that society for material support, and that this explains the allowance of a certain range of leeway to facilitate the smooth interaction of the two worlds.

The Coexistence of Sects

Normally, all monks in a monastery are of the same sect and perform rituals according to the liturgy of that sect. There are exceptions to this rule, however, particularly in the diaspora of refugees outside Tibet. Thus in the Urgyen Gonpa in Bodhnath, also known as Ka-nying Shedrup Ling, there are two tulku of different sects. They are brothers, but the elder brother is a reincarnation of a Kagyupa lama, whereas the younger is the reincarnation of a Nyingmapa lama. The elder brother manages the monastery although in his last reincarnation he was of lower status than his younger brother, who is the reincarnation of a monk of higher status. Because of this split in the leadership, both Kagyupa and Nyingmapa rites are performed within the Urgyen Gonpa and both Kagyupa and Nyingmapa monks reside in the gonpa. The differences between Kagyupa and Nyingmapa liturgies are so slight that Kagyupa and Nyingmapa rituals can be performed in the same gonpa, and monks of both sects can share a single monastery.

Urgyen Tulku Rinpoche was from La-tshap Gonpa in Tibet, and his elder son, Cho-kyinyima Rinpoche, was from Dong Gonpa near Lhasa. The original Tibetan gonpa of his younger son, Chok-ling Rinpoche who is Nyingmapa, was Nangchin Tsiki Gonpa in Kham. Chok-ling Rinpoche is a higher reincarnation than his brother because his previous reincarnation was closer to Guru Rinpoche (Padmasambhava). The eighty monks in the Urgyen gonpa in 1985 included Tibetans, Sherpas, Manangis, Newars and Bhotias from Yelambu. The performance of rituals according to Kagyupa and Nyingmapa liturgies did not cause any problems with so mixed a community.

Within the Kagyupa sect there are the three subdivisions: Karmapa, Drikungpa and Drukpa. Although monks sharing the same monastic community may adhere to any of these divisions, their distinct orientations do not affect their common loyalty to the community of their gonpa.

Similarly, there are three distinct divisions within the Sakyapa sect which do not jeopardize the unity of the monastic community of any specific gonpa. Yet, the structure of the Sakyapa sect is reflected in the administration of

Sakyapa monasteries. Succession to the headship of a Sakyapa monastery is not determined by reincarnation as it is in the case of Gelukpa and Nyingmapa gonpa. The head of the Sakyapa sect, who is known as *gongma,* is never a tulku because there is no process of reincarnation to provide the community with a new head. The Sakya gongma is not expected to be reincarnated, but rather normally marries in order to produce a legitimate son who would succeed him. His wife need not be of high status or even born into a Sakya family.

There are two ruling lineages *(doonggyue)* in the Sakya sect, called Phuntsok Phodang and Dolma Phodang. The present head of the sect belongs to the latter lineage. As gongma he is not necessarily succeeded by his son, as his successor may be a member of the other lineage if there is a man of suitable age and ability. This system assures a balance and no rivalry between the two lineages. Other Sakya abbots who do not belong to either of the two ruling lineages may be reincarnated, and they, as well as ordinary Sakya lamas, may not marry but rather lead a celibate life.

The special character of the Sakya sect, and particularly the system of succession independent of reincarnation, is partly explicable by the historical development of the Sakya community. The first Sakya monastery was founded about 1073 A.D. in the Tsang region of central Tibet. Sakya princes subsequently ruled over an autonomous state situated within central Tibet but not subject to the Dalai Lama's government. The two separate lineages which today alternately provide the gongma as head of the sect may well have been derived from two branches of the ruling family which wielded secular power. The independent Sakya principality embraced several enclaves within the territories of other rulers, and also extended to some valleys of eastern Tibet.

Tibetans living outside Tibet recognize the great importance of monasteries to the survival of Tibetan culture and the preservation of Mahayana Buddhism. Thus, a notable scholar and collaborator of the anthropologist C. Goldstein, Paljor Tsering, outlines in *The Tibet Journal* (1985) the aims of Tibetan monasticism as follows:

> Tibetan monasticism represents one of human history's most ambitious and radical social and psychological experiments precisely because it attempts to achieve on a mass scale the creation and perpetuation of a subculture and society in which basic ideals of non-attachment, non-desire, material renunciation, celibacy and transcendental wisdom are institutionalized. Tibetan history in fact can be conceptualized as the 'monasticization' of a society in that the primary goal of the polity becomes precisely the production and reproduction of as many monks as possible. Lay people exist to serve monasticism by producing sons and (economic) surplus.

Drikung Kyabgon Chetsang, head of the Drikung Kagyu Order
of Buddhism, who walked from Tibet to Nepal in 1975

9

Interviews with Lamas from Tibet

Ato Rinpoche

Tsewang Samten Ato was born in 1933 as the second of ten children, having four brothers and five sisters. His father, Kunchong Lhasung Ato, was the hereditary chieftain of several thousand families in the Ato district of Kham. His mother, Tashi Tsomo, was of a noble family in the principality of Derge in eastern Tibet.

At the early age of four years Tsewang Samten was recognized as the reincarnation (tulku) of a Kagyupa lama. When he was eight, he was sent to the Nezang Gonpa, the family monastery, one day's journey from his father's house where he received the usual monastic education of a novice. In addition to study of religious texts, he specialized in the study of meditation and yoga. For three years, three months and three days he stayed in a solitary retreat. Like his family, he was broadminded and was interested in studying the doctrines of the Sakyapa, Nyingmapa, and Gelukpa sects in addition to Kagyupa doctrine. Following is Ato Rinpoche's personal account of his life history:

> "When I was about eighteen years old, the Chinese wanted to convert the youth of Tibet to their ideology and way of life. Together with other youths of eastern Tibet I was taken to Peking, Shanghai and Nanking in order to become familiar with China. Our monk's robes were taken away, and we were dressed in ordinary Chinese coats and trousers. We were taken to a school where Chinese instructors spoke of Tibetan customs and Buddhist religion with scorn. They tried to force us to give up Buddhist beliefs. Thus I was called upon to denounce the offerings of butter as fuel in lamps at rituals, and was urged to describe this practice as waste. When I contradicted the

teachers and spoke up for Buddhism, I was given the punishment of standing for hours with a heavy log on my head in front of the whole class. Other young lamas who resisted the indoctrination of the Chinese teachers were also severely punished and suffered a great deal.

Then I asked for permission to go home and visit my family. Finally a holiday was sanctioned, but we were told to spread in our home villages the ideology we had been taught

When I reached home, I warned my father that the Chinese communists were very dangerous and that conditions in eastern Tibet would soon become intolerable. I decided not to go back to China, but to go to Lhasa for religious studies. My determination impressed my parents and they agreed to also go to Lhasa, which was then still possible. In Lhasa I studied in the monastery of the Karmapa Lama, and spent one year there completing my study of the Kagyupa doctrine. Because I wanted to also learn Gelukpa scriptures and rituals, I went also to a college of Sera monastery and studied there.

When news of the troubles in eastern Tibet reached Lhasa, my father said that he wanted to go back to Kham and assist the people of his village and monastery in their dealings with the Chinese. Again and again I warned my father of the danger of returning to his home, and advised him and my brothers to remain in Lhasa. But they felt obliged to return in this time of crisis, and all three of them started for our village traveling with yak. I stayed behind in Lhasa continuing my studies at a college of Sera monastery.

Then the fight against the Chinese occupation troops began. My friends and I went to the Dalai Lama's Norbulingkha palace. The Chinese began with their bombing raids and the news from the east became very bad. So I felt that I had to follow my father and my brothers. One night I managed to slip away and went first to Bera and then to Pempo. There I got a horse which enabled me to catch up with my father and brothers. We proceeded together, but our caravan was spotted by a Chinese plane and Chinese troops attacked us. My father and two brothers and also one of my sisters were captured, but I succeeded in escaping and went into hiding.

As an aristocrat and, in Chinese eyes, a 'feudal reactionary' my father was imprisoned, and he was continuously beaten and kicked in jail until he died. My two brothers and one sister were also killed by the Chinese. Now I have no more relations, except one young sister who had stayed behind in our village and had lived with an aunt.

When I heard that the Dalai Lama had managed to escape to India, and I was the only surviving male member of my family, I decided to flee to India. The Chinese had sealed all the easy routes so I had to make a detour looking for unguarded passes. I traveled towards the east as far as the Tsari region, which adjoins the Indian territory then known as Northeast Frontier Agency and now called Arunachal Pradesh. For three weeks I trekked through pathless mountains and bamboo jungles, and in some places the trees were so high and the forest so dense that I could not see the sky for days. Walking in rain through mud and dripping jungle, my companions and I could never dry our clothes and we suffered much from the heat, humidity and bites of countless leeches. In the end we emerged at an Indian outpost near the tribal village of Daporijo, not far from the Subansiri River.

There we stayed for some weeks until the Government of India arranged for a transport plane which took us to Gauhati in Assam. At that time other refugees had crossed the Indian frontier in the Tawang area and had come to Assam via Bomdila.

The Dalai Lama's organization arranged for me to go to Darjeeling, Kalimpong and Sikkim. The Karmapa Lama, the head of the Kagyupa sect, then sent me to Dharamsala where I was to join the Council for Religious Affairs as Representative of the Kagyupa sect. For three years I worked in Dharamsala in that capacity, and from there I went to Dalhousie. I had asked the Religious Affairs office to enable me to learn English, for many Westerners began coming to Dharamsala and I wanted to be able to tell them about Buddhism.

At Dalhousie there was a 'Young Lamas High School' in which English was taught by British volunteers. It was decided that I should learn English in this school. The Dalai Lama then appointed me administrative head of this school, which he wanted to turn into a monastery for young refugees of all the four Tibetan sects.

A parallel school for Tibetan girls was turned into a nunnery. There were English teachers in this school, and as I wanted to marry one of them I told the Dalai Lama of our plans and said that I would have to give up my position as a monk and head of the monastery school. He was very understanding and said that although he regretted my intention of giving up my career as a monk, he appreciated my frankness and the way in which this was done openly without my trying to remain head of the monastery.

Finally I got married, my wife remaining a Christian and I a Buddhist. We went to England and I found work in a hospital in Cambridge, where we now live.

In 1985 I went to eastern Tibet with the permission of the Chinese authorities. I wanted to see my relatives and friends who had survived the Cultural Revolution. I found that none of my brothers and other male relatives were alive. Two of my sisters were still living near my old home. My family's house and also my monastery had been totally destroyed. During that visit I went to see fourteen monasteries in Nangchen. All these had been pulled down, and when I asked the Chinese local authorities whether I could organize the rebuilding of my old monastery, they said that later on permission might be obtained, but just now the local authorities were not empowered to permit the rebuilding of monasteries.

Wherever I went, the local Tibetans received me most cordially and hundreds of people gathered to meet me. They all spoke with the greatest affection and respect for His Holiness the Dalai Lama. 'It is only due to him that we are all right,' they all said. 'If he were not there outside Tibet, we would all be lost.'

That is the general feeling in Tibet. People know that if the Dalai Lama returned to Tibet, he would no longer have his freedom of action."

The Former Abbot of Sok-tenchendengo Gonpa in Tibet

"Sok-tenchendengo Gonpa is situated between Kham and Tsangba. Before the Chinese invasion of Tibet, I studied in Sera Gonpa having been recognized as a reincarnation (tulku). After I had graduated from Sera-Jey (Jey College of Sera monastery), I returned to my own monastery of Sok-tenchendengo in 1959. At that time there were five hundred and fifty monks in the monastery. Then the Chinese attacked the monastery — first with artillery, then by dropping bombs from planes. Twenty monks were killed by these bombs and many of the buildings were destroyed. Three hundred monks were captured by the Chinese soldiers. I myself escaped capture, for when the monastery was attacked and bombed I fled to Tsera-pempa, a place where a number of monks had collected and were joined by Khampas who were prepared to fight the Chinese.

The monks captured at Sok-tenchendengo were sent to a prison-camp at Nagchuka, a provincial centre. There had been no judicial process, but all the monks who had not managed to flee were herded together and sent to the prison-camp, which contained some eight thousand people. The prisoners were forced to work in a mine, where six thousand prisoners died of starvation as they were not given adequate food. About sixty percent of the inmates of the camp were monks, and the others were laymen, mainly of upper class status. Among these were women and adolescents and who were also forced to work. The camp of Nagchuka was dissolved in 1962 and the surviving prisoners were sent to their home regions and imprisoned there.

When Tsera-pempa was surrounded by Chinese soldiers I had succeeded to flee once more and I tried to hide in my home village Tsethang. I was captured there by Chinese and sent to prison in Pachendong where the prisoners had to work very hard for ten hours a day, building houses and working on the land. The crops grown on the fields were all taken by the Chinese, and the prisoners received only five hundred grams tsampa and two hundred-fifty grams each of tea and butter per month.

In 1975 I was sent to a prison in Lhasa where ten prisoners shared one small room. They were not allowed to talk to prisoners of another room and they had to queue for going to a latrine. If a prisoner was heard to say any prayer such as *om mani padme hum,* he was beaten. The Chinese forced other prisoners to beat the culprit, and soldiers too beat the prisoners as punishment for any such offense however minor. Anybody complaining about the inadequacy of rations was also beaten. Sometimes the Chinese forced the prisoners to curse the Dalai Lama and to accuse him of all sorts of misdeeds. Whoever refused to do so was tortured. There were separate prisons for women and they too were treated cruelly.

I was altogether seventeen years in prison, the reason being my position as reincarnate abbot of Sok-tenchendengo Gonpa. In 1977, I was released and allowed to live in Lhasa. But until 1979 I had to stay in a police compound and work in a car workshop. To leave the compound and walk about in Lhasa I had to get special permission. At that time I was given a monthly wage of thirty-seven yuan (which corresponded then about fourteen and a half dollars). After 1979 the salary was raised to one hundred and eight yuan per month, and after working hours I was allowed to walk about Lhasa without special permission.

In 1980 there was a change of policy and most political prisoners were freed. A year later I obtained permission to go to Nepal. I came here alone, but twenty monks of my monastery had already escaped in 1969 — two of them had come to Kathmandu while others had gone to Dharamsala and others to a Tibetan settlement in Karnataka.

In January 1985 some of the monks who had remained in Tibet started to rebuild the Sok-tenchen monastery. Old monks who were over sixty years of age were allowed to stay in the monastery, but younger monks had to work for the Chinese in order to obtain food.

The lay people in my village could cultivate their land, but if they expressed any political opinion, such as saying 'Tibet should be free,' they were punished. Some Tibetans have regained their original positions in the local administration, but the Chinese have all the power and make all the decisions.

It depends on the Chinese policies whether I shall ever return to Tibet. If the Chinese grant the Tibetans their freedom, I myself and many other lamas are likely to return, but under present conditions I would not consider such a move.

The Chinese administration does not directly interfere in the monasteries, but the village headmen, who are Tibetans, do interfere and they are responsible to Chinese. The district head *(chikhyab)* who controls the *dzong* is always Chinese. The *dzongpon* (official in charge of the district) may be a Tibetan and the village headmen are Tibetans. But dzongpon and headmen cannot make decisions without referring to the Chinese."

Gyalsey Rinpoche of Deru-Sandup Choling Gonpa

"My family's home is in Hor Yeta. We were five brothers, and three of these, including myself, were reincarnations. I myself am the reincarnation of a Sakyapa lama, but two of my brothers are Kagyupa tulku and my second brother is a Bönpo reincarnation, and was originally claimed by a Bönpo monastery. Now, however, he lives in Bir in India.

At the time of the Chinese invasion, all of us left Tibet. That was in 1959 and we all, including my father, headed towards Mustang but reached it by different routes. I was then only nine years of age but I remember our arrival in Mustang very distinctly. We had some yak with us and had also brought some rifles, and some ornaments and precious stones. The lamas of the various gonpa of Mustang did not help us much with provisions for they did not have much to eat themselves, and there were many refugees including numerous reincarnations. So we had to sell our possessions in order to buy food. The rifles and ornaments were bought by rich Mustang families who did not give us fair prices. I myself found shelter in the small monastery of Lo-Gekar near Tsarang, and stayed there for one year.

From there I went with some lamas to Kathmandu, and stayed there for two months. Next I went with a group of refugees to Darjeeling, and there we met the Dalai Lama's secretary. Though there were thousands of Tibetan refugees in Darjeeling, he arranged for our stay and maintenance.

My mother had died in Tibet and my father, who had reached India, died there. Two of my brothers went to north India, and I was taken care of by the Dalai Lama's organization and settled with other refugees in Bir. There the Tibetans have some cultivable land and keep a few cows and sheep. They are also engaged in carpet making and do some minor trade with Tibet.

In my old monastery Deru-Sandup Choling there are nowadays only some thirty-five monks. In 1982 two elder brothers of mine went to Tibet, but only one of them has stayed there. The other had come back to India."

The family of Gyalsey Rinpoche is unusual in the sense that the five brothers belong to different sects. Of the three tulku two were reincarnations of Kagyupa lamas, and when the eldest was recognized as the reincarnation of the abbot of a Kagyupa gonpa in Kham, the whole family moved to Nangchen. But when the second brother was claimed as tulku of a Bönpo gonpa in central Tibet, his parents refused to give him up for education as a Bönpo lama and he is now a Kagyupa layman and not a Bönpo reincarnate abbot. The third brother, known as Antoul Rinpoche, is a Kagyupa tulku and has a gonpa at Rewalsar in India. Although he is a tulku, he is married.

Alan Arora

The late Senior Tutor to the Dalai Lama leading a prayer ceremony in Dharamsala, India

The Wheel of Life thanka painting by Renchen Norbu

10

The Role of Art

ENDEAVOURS OF TIBETAN refugee communities to counteract the Chinese policy of destroying Buddhist culture and ideology throughout the Tibetan heartland are not confined to the preservation of traditional religious beliefs and practices of the four sects of Buddhism and parallel spiritual developments among the adherents of the ancient Bön religion. Restoration of these religious values by teaching of the doctrine also has the by-product of cultivating the visual arts which pass on the complex structure of Tibetan Buddhism in all its aspects to future generations.

Traditionally, Buddhist ideas have frequently been expressed in artistic creation — paintings on gonpa walls as well as the sacred scrolls hanging in temples and private chapels provide one of the most effective tools of transmitting Buddhist concepts to the laity. Indeed, thanka painters were usually very well versed in Buddhist teaching.

Refugee communities, however poor in material resources, made strenuous efforts to recreate the outward symbols of Buddhism by building chorten and mani-walls, raising prayer flags, and finally constructing gonpas. The latter serve as focal points of Buddhist community life and — through their frescoes and statues — provide a vivid introduction to Buddhist mythology, history and doctrine understandable even to the untutored laymen and helpful for the teaching of basic religious concepts.

The Tibetan religious urge was so strong that it overcame all material obstacles. Monks collected funds and wealthy business men donated building sites and cash, while even the relatively poor contributed at least a few rupees. Monks helped with the building work where necessary, and laymen vied with each other in supporting each project. Even poorly educated Tibetans instinctively felt that the efforts of artists were essential in recreating the visual forms in which their faith and tradition could flourish.

Biography of a Traditional Thanka Painter

Renchen Norbu was born in 1941 in the city of Tao in far eastern Tibet on the borders of China. His full name is Datsong Choinze Renchen Norbu Ranyubu. As it was customary for wealthy young noblemen to receive education in the gonpa, he spent nine years along with seven thousand lamas at Drepung gonpa in Lhasa. He studied the five inner knowledges consisting of the precepts of Buddhist teachings and the five outer knowledges dealing with mathematics, medicine and art. He gained the title of *Datsang Choinze* (One of Learned Accomplishments).

After escaping Tibet in 1959 and spending a year in Kalimpong, he went to Darjeeling and became the assistant editor and circulation manager of the Tibetan Freedom Press. Here he met and studied with the master painter Lhbri Targay of the Karma Kagyu lineage whose style of painting is known as Karma Kabri. One of the main characteristics of this style of painting is the dot shading technique. This method gives a sense of atmosphere and depth to the portrayal of the five elements of air, earth, fire, water and ether.

In 1976 Renchen came to Nepal and began painting full time. His work has mainly been for monasteries and practising Buddhists. In autumn of 1981, with a group of eight students, he began work on a series of frescoes for the Hotel Vajra. Created using the traditional technique of embossing the design — coupled with Renchen's choice of subject and excellent execution of the work — these frescoes are an outstanding example of contemporary Tibetan painting. The work took four months to complete.

Robert Hahn

Gonpa interior in Khumbu with traditional thanka paintings

Above: Fresco in Sakya gonpa in Bodhnath
Opposite: Detail of Tibetan painted ceiling at Hotel Vajra in Kathmandu by Renchen Norbu

Bodhnath stupa with prayer flags

11

Monasteries at Bodhnath

THE GREAT STUPA of Bodhnath in Nepal has been a centre of Buddhist worship attracting pilgrims from Tibet, Ladakh, Bhutan, Sikkim and many of the outlying Buddhist regions of Nepal for centuries. No major monasteries were located in its vicinity, however, until recently. A chapel *(lhakhang)* in the house of a lama popularly known as the Chini Lama — because he was supposed to have come from China — was the only place designed for the performance of Buddhist rites.

Ganden Chendeling gonpa, the first Tibetan monastery established at Bodhnath, is generally known as the 'Mongolian gonpa' because the founder Sokur Gurdeva was a Mongolian who came to Nepal from Mongolia in the 1950s. Some pious person gave him a piece of land where he built a small hut. Later, he was given more land and built a larger house. Gradually obtaining more land from private persons, Sokur Rinpoche completed the present gonpa in 1959 and it has since been further enlarged.

There were more Tibetans than Mongolians among the sixteen monks with whom Sokur Rinpoche started the monastery. By 1985 the number of monks had risen to seventy, many of whom had come from Sandling Gonpa in Tibet after the 1959 diaspora. Thirty or forty monks came from other monasteries in Tibet, but all they could bring with them were a few books.

The founder put the gonpa at the disposal of the Dalai Lama, who named it Ganden Chendeling Gonpa and gave it to the care of the Sera, Ganden and Drepung monastery branches recently established in Karnataka. These monasteries provide administrators or abbots (khanpo) in rotation for the gonpa, each khanpo having a tenure of five years. Ngawang Ngendra, a *geshe* (a high academic degree equivalent to a doctorate in theology), held the position of khanpo in 1985. Sokur Rinpoche, the founder, was then at the Drepung Gonpa at Mundgod in Karnataka in south India. Chendeling Gonpa has no cultivable land and no regular income from donors but is nevertheless self-supporting. The present monks are all Tibetans; there are no Sherpas or Newars among them.

Thrangu Tashi Choling Gonpa (Kagyupa) is a small gonpa built like an ordinary dwelling and stands behind the inner circle of houses surrounding the stupa of Bodhnath. It was built in 1976 by Thrangu Tulku Rinpoche who had come from Thrangu Tashi Choling Gonpa in Kyigodo (Jyekundo) in Kham province in Tibet, from which he had fled to Lhasa with twenty monks. With ten of these monks, he went to Bhutan and then to Nepal, where they founded the gonpa. The site was purchased with personal funds of the tulku, augmented by some local donations and contributions from Western disciples. The gonpa contains a Buddha statue which is nine and a half feet high and was specifically made to fit into the main hall of the gonpa. Thrangu Tulku acts as *loben* (senior cleric conducting ritual performances) and there are also such officials as umse, nierwa, chorpen and chutimba. The community of monks includes Newars, Manangis, Tamangs and novices from local Tibetan families, in addition to the original immigrants from Tibet. All rites are performed according to the Kagyupa liturgy.

Kargon-tine-chunkorle Gonpa (Kagyupa) is a small gonpa standing on a site donated by the Chini Lama among houses encircling the Bodhnath stupa. The founder, Dabsang Rinpoche, is a Tibetan tulku who walked from Lo-Manthang (Mustang) to Kathmandu in 1959 with Sechu Rinpoche and nine monks after they had all fled from Dyilyag Gonpa in Nangchen in Kham in Tibet. Sechu Rinpoche, another tulku, was given a house at Swayambunath and placed in charge of the gonpa there (see Chapter 12).

In 1982 Dabsang visited Tibet where he found his original gonpa in Nangchen totally destroyed. During the invasion, the Chinese not only destroyed most of the gonpa buildings but also smashed most statues and

Ganden monastery

confiscated the land and livestock which belonged to the monastery. Some of the old monks were alive and still perform certain rites in a small gonpa which they had built on part of the site.

A few novices in the Kargon-tine-chunkorla Gonpa are from among the Tibetan population settled in the Nepal Valley. In 1985 there were thirty-eight monks — about sixty percent Tibetans, some Sherpa, some from Yelmu and some from Bhutan. The monks have some contact with monasteries in Karnataka.

Sakya Monasteries at Bodhnath

The Tsechen Shedupling Gonpa was built in 1969 by Tarig Rinpoche, a tulku who came from Tarig Gonpa Rashu in one of the outer districts of Nangchen in Kham, Tibet. He and seven of his monks fled Tibet in 1959 and entered Nepal via Lo-Manthang (Mustang), having stayed there for a year before going to Dhorpatan where they built a small gonpa.

They moved to Bodhnath, where the Chini Lama gave them a building site of three hundred square feet to which they added land purchased with funds collected from the local population and Buddhists in other parts of Nepal.

The gonpa founded by Tarig Rinpoche is a large building complex consisting of a sumptuously decorated hall (dukhang) with fine frescoes, a porch, refectory, a library situated in a separate building, and an apartment

Sakya Gonpa (1986)

and chapel for the abbot which are situated above the dukhang. Two large wings provide accommodation for monks.

In 1985 there were sixty monks recruited from local Tibetan families, Mustang and Manang. The monks maintained themselves by casual donations and earnings derived from performance of rituals at the invitation of private persons. Numerous young novices learn reading and writing in the monastery, and are then sent to other schools and monasteries for further instruction. It is planned that all stages of instruction will soon be provided in the gonpa at Bodhnath.

Besides the Tulku Tarig Rinpoche, a young tulku also resides in the gonpa. He was born at Bodhnath and recognized as a reincarnation of a lama of Tarig Gonpa in Tibet which was completely demolished by the Chinese. There used to be three tulku in Tarig Gonpa, and one of them was still in Tibet in 1983. In 1982 Tarig Rinpoche ventured to return there where he found about twenty monks still living in the vicinity. With their help and the assistance of some local villagers, Tarig Rinpoche undertook the task of restoring part of the gonpa. More than one hundred monks had lived in Tarig Gonpa, but most had been killed by the Chinese.

At Tarig Rinpoche's monastery at Bodhnath, orientation at summer solstice places the entrance due south, the altar is at the north end, and the monks face east and west. The main hall is rectangular with the length running north to south. As is traditional, a beautiful portico at the entrance is approached by a few stairs.

The portico walls are richly painted with numerous frescoes. Following the tradition, most of these frescoes can be found at the entrance to any Sakya monastery. Indeed, some can be found at the entrance to every monastery, such as the 'Guardians of the Four Cardinal Directions' who are portrayed with terrifying faces or purposefully riding their mounts to protect the gonpa from enemies of the *dharma* (Buddhist way of life). Another painting, left of the entrance, is the *Wheel of Life,* considered the oldest thanka and which embraces the most basic ideas of Buddhism within it.

The *Wheel of Life* is a reminding factor to all who enter the lhakhang that the aim is to get off the wheel of suffering and recurrence which is spun by three animals at the centre: the pig which represents ignorance, the cock which represents lust and greed, and the snake which represents envy and hate. Around the hub are depicted those who through right action are ascending, and those who through wrong action are led downward. Between the spokes of the wheel are the six realms into which one can be incarnated through these actions. At the bottom is hell or purgatory, in the lower right the region of the hungry ghosts or *preta,* in the lower left the animal realm, in the upper left the realm of man, in the upper right the realm of the titans or demigods, and in the top the realm of the gods. Each realm has its own suffering, none are exempt. In each, also, can be seen a manifestation of Lord

Buddha, who can lead one out of the realm. The rim of the wheel is divided into twelve, signifying the twelve occurrences from conception to separation after death. Holding the wheel is the Lord of the Dead.

One painting in this gonpa is not traditional and it is delightful. If one were to look to the south from the entrance on the upper wall there is shown a gathering of people coming to the stupa. In it are seen Tibetans, one with a camera, Nepalis, and a Western lady and gentleman — a humorous showing of Buddhism in our contemporary times.

Jobche Trichen Gonpa was built at Bodhnath by the head of the Tsarpa branch of the Sakya sect. His old monastery is at Lumbini in Nepal and some monks of Lumbini commute between Lumbini and the new gonpa at Bodhnath, which they apparently helped to build. Accommodation for visiting monks from Lumbini are provided in the basement. On October 9, 1985 the head of the whole Sakya sect, Trizen Rinpoche, performed a blessing ceremony *(rapne)* for the gonpa, assisted by monks of Lumbini and Tsechen Shedupling Gonpa of Bodhnath.

A third Sakya monastery is being built at Bodhnath behind the Tsechen Shedupling Gonpa. The founder, Deshung Rinpoche, owned a monastery in Tibet. In 1985 he lived in the United States but a khanpo and some monks of the Tibetan monastery are supervising the construction. Most of the finance was being provided by the Deshung Rinpoche. The new monastery will contain numerous living quarters for monks and pilgrims visiting the Sakya gonpa of Bodhnath.

Dancers at blessing ceremony for the nearly completed Tsechen Shedupling Gonpa

12

Monasteries at Swayambunath

THE ANCIENT STUPA of Swayambunath — with a pair of watchful eyes gazing to each of the four cardinal directions — rises over the Kathmandu landscape on the hill of Swayambu. Five Tibetan monasteries, three Gelukpa and two Kagyupa, have recently been built at this legendary site whose exact date of origin is buried in antiquity.

Karma Randa Mahabal Gonpa stands next to the large and venerated stupa at Swayambunath. Darma Lama, who was a Kagyupa and a geshe from Dangma Chungling in Tibet, founded the gonpa. He built a lhakhang, later giving it as a gift to Karmapa Lama whom he asked to stay there as his representative. Subsequently, Karmapa gave the lhakhang to Sechu Rimpoche, who came to Nepal from Diylyag Gonpa in Nangchen accompanied by twenty monks in 1959. They crossed into Nepal at Mustang where they had stayed for one year before coming to Swayambunath.

In 1985 there were fifty monks in the gonpa — Newaris, Manangis and Sherpas, in addition to the Tibetan refugee monks — whose support came from donations and fees for performance of rituals for private customers. Debates and examinations in this gonpa are not the same as they were in Tibet. Young novices are sent to Rumtek in Sikkim for studies.

Ganden Jam Ghon Ling gonpa was under repair in 1985. A Newar Uday pearl trader called Bodiratna Tulada, who had spent some time in Tibet and took an interest in religious buildings, sponsored the construction which began in 1954. Initially a small building, the gonpa was virtually knocked down in 1983 and rebuilt much larger. In 1985 it was decorated with new frescoes with the help of donations collected locally and from American and European devotees.

There were eight Newari monks at Ganden Jam Ghon Ling gonpa when it was first built. In 1959 Serkong Dorje Chang. a tulku from Ganden Gonpa in Tibet, came to Swayambunath with twenty monks. At first Serkong Dorje Chang and his Tibetan monks stayed close to Swayambunath in the old gonpa

(Karma Randa Mahabal) and at that time the Gelukpa and Kagyupa monks lived together, but this caused friction. The Newari monks then invited the Gelukpa monks and the tulku to move to Ganden Jam Ghon Ling although it was not yet entirely completed.

In 1983 the gonpa had been almost completely rebuilt. The architect was Dorjela, a Tibetan from Darjeeling who was also a very skilled woodcarver. A Tibetan painter did the decorations.

Some of the Tibetan monks came from Kham, having gone to Kailash and then to Nepal and ultimately arriving at Swayambunath. Some monks came from Ganden, some from Drepung and some from Sera monasteries in Tibet. The Ganden Jam Ling Gonpa has a *Kagyur* (teachings attributed to the historical Buddha) and other valuable books which the monks had brought from Tibet before the Chinese invasion.

Tulku Serkong Dorje Chang died in 1968 and was reborn in India at Kollegar in Mysore. The present incarnation was five years old in 1985 and it was believed that he would be enthroned and brought to Swayambunath in 1986.

Thukje Choling Gonpa lies on Saraswati Hill above the Ganden Jam Gon Ling Gonpa. It was founded by Thukje Rinpoche who came from Lhasa in 1963 and holds the position of khenpo. He was originally in Drepung Loselling, and spent three years in a Chinese prison. He came to Nepal via Sikkim and stayed some time in Kalimpong. In 1985 there were about fifty-five monks in the gonpa, fifty of whom were Tibetans, while some are Bhotias from the region of Gosainkund in Nepal.

Dharma Chakra Gonpa, an older monastery located nearby, was built in 1940 by Sherpruk Rinpoche who had come from Kham. He died in 1960 and had left instructions that the gonpa be given to Thukje Rinpoche. Sherpruk Rinpoche had not yet been reincarnated in 1985.

Thukje Rinpoche had been invited by Chatura, a Newar of Asan Tol, and stayed in meditation below Swayambunath for about two years. Though Sherpruk's gonpa had been given to him, Thukje Rinpoche built a new gonpa in 1973, and many poor people contributed their labour to the construction work. The new gonpa was designed by a Nepali architect but the top, which is in pagoda style, is a replica of buildings in Lhasa.

In a cluster of houses below Swayambunath, in 1982 the Manangi community built a gonpa named after Pemba Tsering, a Member of Parliament, who had the idea of building the gonpa and donated the building site. There are no lamas or monks in the gonpa, but two nuns from Manang act as *konier* (sacristan), maintaining the services of burning lamps and changing the water in the altar bowls. A Manangi lama is called from his gonpa in Pokhara for the performance of any major rite, as this lama looks after both this gonpa and that of Pokhara. The Manangis who live in Kathmandu sometimes assemble in the gonpa and perform a *puja* (prayer ceremony). In the month of February all the Manangis gather there and recite the prayer *"om mani padme hum"* for some million times. This takes up to fifteen days.

Nyenam Phelgyeling Gonpa (Gelukpa) is named after a gonpa in Tibet, near Kotari and close to the border of Nepal, from which most of the monks came. Thirty-seven of the approximately fifty monks in that gonpa left Tibet together with the Umze Lobsang Phande. After crossing the Nepalese border, they first went to Barabise and stayed at the Phegung Gonpa, and then for some time at the Tashi Gonpa at Bigu. From there they went to the Bhakhang Gonpa in Yelambu and where they stayed for about a year. All that time they moved together from place to place. From Bhakhang they came to Kindo near Swayambu. From Kindo they went to the Jeta Bahal in Patan for a year, where they were welcomed by a Newar monk with whom they had been acquainted. Afterwards they moved to the Anankuti Bahal at Swayamkuti, where there were many Hinayana monks and lived there for some time.

Many Tibetans settled in the Kathmandu Valley then approached them and offered them donations to build a monastery of their own. They accepted this proposal and collected additional funds. When they had sufficient money, they bought a site for thirty thousand rupees and spent one hundred thousand rupees on a building. The monks themselves also helped build and decorate the dukhang into which they laced two statues — one of Dolma (the patron goddess of Tibet who represents the motherly aspect of compassion) and one of Milarepa — which they had brought from Tibet and carried with them on their long migration from gonpa to gonpa. The gonpa has a large courtyard where the monks performed Cham dances similar to those enacted at Mani-Rimdu rites.

The Nyenam Phelgyeling Gonpa monks also plan to build a meditation hall behind Swayambunath for which they have already acquired a site.

Cham dance at Nyenam Penjeling Gonpa

13

The Installation of a New Tulku

IN NOVEMBER 1985 the largest Sakya gonpa at Bodhnath was the scene of the solemn installation of a new Sakya tulku. The centre of the celebration was a boy of twelve years of age, whose Tibetan parents were living close to Bodhnath. He had been recognized as the reincarnation of Yoten Tulku, a lama in the Tarig Gonpa of Tibet. There had been three tulku in the Tarig Gonpa. One is Tarig Rinpoche, the present abbot of the Tsechen Shedupling Gonpa at Bodhnath, and one who still lives at Tarig in Nangchen in Tibet. Yonten Tulku was the third tulku, and he was now reincarnated in the young boy to be installed in the Sakya gonpa at Bodhnath.

In the morning of the eleventh of November, a large crowd of Tibetans — consisting of all Sakya lamas who had been within reach and a number of lay people who had received personal invitations because they were acquainted with the family of the new tulku or with the abbot or other dignitaries of the gonpa — assembled at Tsechen Shedupling Gonpa. There were at least hundred monks of all ages, wearing red and yellow garments. Among the lay-folk were men in typical Tibetan clothes, some looking rather unkempt and ragged, and some in smart Nepali or Western dress. The women wore clothes of Tibetan style, though modern machine-made textiles in pastel colours had replaced the coarser handwoven Tibetan material in some cases. Many women wore heavy Tibetan ornaments of silver, coral, turquoise and various semi-precious stones.

A large round tent had been put up on the lawn next to the gonpa, where a variety of Tibetan and Nepalese dishes were served to all those invited to the celebration. There was sufficient food and drink to provide for eventual gate-crashers.

The guests soon drifted from this tent into the gonpa to watch the enthronement rite *(Thridon Zego)*. The abbot sat on his high chair close to the altar, and the young new tulku was seated on a cushion on the floor opposite the seat of the abbot. The latter then recited words of purification

The abbot and new tulku exchange bows of respect

while sprinkling water on the young tulku, thus ceremoniously cleansing him. Next the abbot handed ritual gifts such as silk scarves *(kata),* sacred books and a *vajra* (thunderbolt symbol) to the umze of the gonpa to be passed on to the new tulku.

The abbot and the umze lifted the young tulku from his cushion on the floor to the throne erected for him to the right side of the altar. Once he was installed on the throne, the tulku of all the monasteries at Bodhnath filed past him and gave him gifts of scarves, books and ritual objects. After these presentations, the people present in the gonpa also went up to the new tulku and offered him ceremonial scarves with some money wrapped up in the silk cloth.

The tulku's parents were seated behind him, and all attending the ceremony also gave them scarves and gifts of money. Similar presents were offered as well to the teacher of the young tulku. While all this was going on, the monks sat on cushions in their usual places along the aisle of the dukhang, chanting and reciting prayers for the long life, good fortune and happiness of the newly installed tulku.

The general opinion was that the boy would receive his further education in the Tsechen Shedupling Gonpa, and ultimately be sent to another Sakya gonpa, possibly in Karnataka, for advanced studies unless conditions improved to such an extent that higher studies in Sakya monasteries in Tibet were again possible.

Enthronement ritual for the new tulku

14

The Bön of Tibet:

The Historical Enigma of a Monastic Tradition

by Per Kværne

BUDDHISM WAS ESTABLISHED in Tibet in the eighth century A.D. Although Tibet at that time had close political and cultural ties with China, it was in its Indian form that the doctrine of the Buddha was introduced into the Land of Snow, and to this day the Tibetans have remained profoundly attached to Buddhism. Over the centuries, an original Buddhist civilization developed in Tibet, a dynamic culture expanding into neighbouring areas like Mongolia and the Himalayas, bringing elements of Indian culture and philosophy to regions as distant as Siberia and southwest China.

The most important feature of this culture was probably the monastic institutions which it produced, eventually developing into immense monastic communities inhabited by thousands of monks.[1] In these monasteries, many features of monastic life, as it was led in India before Buddhism disappeared in its land of origin, were preserved. The most significant contribution of this monastic tradition to human culture was the faithful translation of the entire Buddhist Sanskrit literature of India into classical Tibetan, surely one of the most impressive intellectual achievements in the history of man. Thus an important aspect of Indian culture was preserved beyond the Himalayas when Buddhism was destroyed in India itself; and, in our own times, Tibetan studies have until fairly recently tended to be regarded as a subordinate but significant discipline of Indology, rather than a field of study in its own right.

The tragic fate of Tibet is well known. In particular, the years of the so-called Cultural Revolution were a period of unparalleled destruction, particularly of monastic institutions and religious texts and objects, as well as of brutal persecution of Tibetan monks and lay people.[2]

Fortunately, Chinese policy has undergone significant changes in recent years. Monasteries are now being rebuilt all over Tibet, and religious life is slowly being reorganized. Outside Tibet, the study of Tibetan history, culture, and religion has developed into an academic discipline in its own right. This is a direct result of the upheavals in Tibet and the subsequent establishment of a Tibetan exile community in India and elsewhere.

A particularly interesting monastic community of the Tibetan diaspora is to be found in the Indian state of Himachal Pradesh, some fifteen kilometres from the town of Solan.[3] The interest of this monastery — the only one of its kind in India — is due to its adherence to a little-known Tibetan tradition. For although the majority of the Tibetans (inside Tibet as well as in exile) are devout Buddhists, a minority — in many parts of Tibet a considerable minority — profess to belong to a distinct religion for which there is no other term than that which the Tibetans themselves use, viz., Bön. The adherents of Bön are known as Bönpos, again using the Tibetan term. Thus in Tibet there are, properly speaking, two religions: Buddhism (which in Tibetan is called Chös) and Bön.[4]

Founded in 1969, the Bönpo monastery in India has been built by the Tibetans themselves virtually without donations from abroad. With great care it has been constructed so as to form an exact replica of a traditional Tibetan monastery, as regards architecture, decorations, and actual monastic life. At present, the monastery has some one hundred and twenty monks. The term 'monk', however, needs clarification. Only a minority are actually fully ordained, observing all the two hundred and fifty-three rules of a *drang-song* (corresponding to the Sanskrit term *rsi),* a term which the Bönpos, for reasons which are not yet entirely clear, use in the place of the Buddhist term *dge-slong* (translating *bhiksu).* About sixty monks are novices, observing only a limited number of rules. Most of these are aged between fifteen and thirty years. The remainder are boys who have been sent to the monastery by their parents in the hope that they will eventually take vows and become fully ordained monks. In the meantime they are taught basic texts, proper behavior, the performance of rituals, etc. The most important group is, perhaps, that constituted by the novices. They are all pupils of a special monastic school offering an eight-year course of intensive study of the philosophical texts of the Bönpos: cosmology, logic, astrology, medicine, poetics, grammar — the full range, in fact, of traditional scholastic subjects. The process of learning is punctuated by debates, in which the students are pitted against each other in a formalized, yet extremely lively exchange of questions and answers. Quick thinking, clarity of expression, and a thorough knowledge of the scriptures from which basic passages must be quoted by heart are required to clinch an argument. The philosophical topics are the same as those of Mahayana Buddhist philosophy — Madhya-mika, Prajnaparamita, logic — but the texts are the Bönpos' own. This eight-year course leads to the degree of *dge-nbshes,* which may be fairly equated with a Ph.D. The first group of six dge-bshes took their final exams in February

1986, and will, it is hoped, spearhead a revival of monastic institutions among Bönpos in Nepal, and eventually perhaps even in Tibet itself.

While Tibetan Buddhism has been studied in India and the West for some 150 years, Bön has, until recently, remained virtually unexplored. In the past, this state of affairs gave rise to highly inadequate theories as to what Bön actually is: the favourite labels were 'animism' and 'shamanism', as it was supposed that all popular religious beliefs and practices which were not specifically Buddhist must of necessity be Bön. On the other hand, it was noted that the Bönpos had monasteries, rituals, scriptures and an iconography very similar, or so it seemed, to that of the Buddhists. Hence it was concluded — rather hastily, as we now begin to realize — that the Bönpos represented a sort of autochthonous reaction to Buddhism, indeed a perversion of Buddhism, a desperate attempt to preserve the ancient, pre-Buddhist traditions by shamelessly plagiarizing the more successful aspects of Buddhism.

The weak point of this theory was, however, that virtually no Bönpo texts were known outside Tibet, nor was any real contact made with Bönpos before the early 1960s. The turning point came with the exodus of Tibetans following the uprising in Lhasa in 1959. Among the Tibetan refugees in India were several highly learned Bönpo scholars who were invited to work with Western scholars in Europe.[6]

One conclusion which was arrived at fairly rapidly was that the texts and the doctrines of the Bön religion could be neither explained nor understood merely by invoking plagiarism. Certainly basic concepts, such as the doc-

Bön monks engaged in debate in monastery courtyard

trines of *karma, samsara,* and *nirvana,* to mention only some key terms, are as fundamental to Bön as they are to Buddhism, and there can hardly be any doubt as to the Indian origin of these concepts. Likewise, ethical norms, meditational practices, scriptural divisions into *sutra* and *tantra* and so on, are the same in Bön and Buddhism. Monastic life and monastic organization are also to a large extent the same, but here the great diversity within Tibetan Buddhist monastic life itself must be borne in mind.

At this point it might well be asked: would it not be proper to regard the Bönpos as a somewhat exotic Tibetan Buddhist school? What does their originality, if any, consist in? It must be conceded that if one insists on answering these questions in terms of doctrine, philosophy, and external practices, one will be hard put to point out significant differences between Bön and Buddhism. However, it is perfectly legitimate to answer the questions from a rather different point of view, viz., in terms of the historical perspective and ultimate legitimation which is regarded as valid *by the believers themselves.* If we adopt this perspective, the following difference between Bön and Buddhism becomes significant: while the ultimate source of authority for Buddhist beliefs and practices is the Buddha Sakyamuni, the Bönpos claim that the true Buddha of our age is not the Indian prince of the Sakya clan, but a different prince, known as sTon-pa gShen-rab, 'gShen-rab the Teacher', who lived in the holy land of 'Ol-mo-lung-ring', also known as 'sTag- gzig', far to the west of Tibet, thousands of years before Sakyamuni. His biography is by no means a mere copy of that of the Buddha, as may be seen from a number of salient features: being an enlightened being from time immemorial, he has no need to obtain enlightenment after his birth among humans; in contrast to Sakyamuni, he teaches a substantial part of his doctrine while still a layman, and his numerous wives and sons play an important role in disseminating the doctrine; he engages in a long drawn-out combat with the Prince of Darkness, the Mara of the Bönpos, who is, however, finally converted and becomes one of his most ardent disciples; after his passing into final *nirvana* his doctrine is written down immediately and spread throughout the world.[7]

The Bönpos further believe that their religion was introduced into Tibet during the reign of the first mythical kings, long before the coming of Buddhism. They thus regard Bön as the true and authentic religion of Tibet, and that it was only after the introduction of Buddhism that Bön was persecuted and subsequently disappeared from many parts of the country; however, the sacred texts were hidden away, to be taken out later when the time was ripe, and thus Bön was revived in the eleventh century, monasteries established, and its continued tradition ensured down to the present day.[8]

By way of conclusion, I would like to suggest certain issues raised by research in the Bön religion.

As we have seen, the Bönpos claim that their religion was established in Tibet and had long had the favour of the kings when Buddhism was introduced from India. It is at present difficult to find external evidence to substantiate this claim. Nevertheless, there were priests in Tibet before the coming of Buddhism, known as Bönpo. The problem is, however, that as far as can be understood from the early sources, there would seem to be only a tenuous link between these Bönpo priests, whose main duty apparently was to perform sacrifices for the benefit of the kings, and the later, lamaist, monastic Bönpo religion. We know all too little about the cultural milieu of Tibet in the seventh and eighth centuries; we are ignorant of the actual nature of the pre-Buddhist religious beliefs of the Tibetans; and we do not know which factors were decisive in ensuring the ultimate triumph of Buddhism.

Whatever the nature of the ancient sacrificial Bönpo priests, it is certain that by the eleventh century a religion, styling itself Bön, was firmly established and has continued to flourish with interruption until today. What is the link between the ancient Bön and the later religion bearing the same name? We do not know; and yet the solution to this mystery might at the same time explain how Tibetan Buddhism and indeed Tibetan society as a whole came to acquire the structure it had by the eleventh or twelfth century, a structure which in many respects remained unchanged until our own century.

Finally, a better understanding of the Bön religion will perhaps shed interesting light on the nature of Buddhism in general. What happens when

The Rev. Sangye Tenzin Youngdong, abbot of the Bönpo monastery in India

118

Buddhism confronts a tenacious autochthonous religion? In many parts of Asia the conflict was resolved by the local religion becoming subordinated to Buddhism, usually to the point of losing any distinctive name. Perhaps what happened in the case of Bön was the Buddhism became *nominally* subordinated to the local religion, losing its name and yet subtly succeeding in permeating the older faith its own values and philosophy? Have other influences — Iranian or Taoist — been at work in the formation of the Bön religion? Only future research will perhaps provide an answer to some of these questions.

NOTES

1. Of a number of recent introductions to the history of Tibetan religion, the following remains the best overall account: D.L. Snellgrove and Hugh E. Richardson, *A Cultural History of Tibet*, (London, 1968; reprint Boulder, Colorado, 1980). A shorter essay is Per Kværne, "Tibet: the Rise and Fall of a Monastic Tradition," pp. 253-270 in H. Bechert and R. Gombrich (eds.), *The World of Buddhism* (London, 1984). A brief introduction is provided by Per Kværne, "Tibetan Religions: An Overview," in Mircea Eliade (ed.), *The Encyclopedia of Religion*, Volume 14, pp. 497- 504 (New York, 1987).

2. A particularly well-documented book covering recent events in Tibet, including outstanding photographic documentation, is Peter-Hannes Lehman and Jay Ullal, *Tibet: Das stille Drama auf dem Dach der Erde* (Hamburg, 1981). John F. Avedon, *In Exile from the Land of Snows* (London, 1984) may also be recommended.

3. Tadeusz Skorupski, "Tibetan g-Yung-drung Bön Monastery at Dolanji," *Kailash* 8,1-2 (1981) pp. 25-43, reprinted in *The Tibet Journal* 11,2 (1986) pp. 36-49.

4. An overview of the Bön religion is S.G. Karmay, "A General Introduction to the History of Doctrines of Bön," in *Memoirs of the Research Department of the Toyo Bunko*, No. 33, (Tokyo, 1975) pp. 171-218. A brief account is provided by Per Kværne, "Bön," in Mircea Eliade (ed.), *The Encyclopedia of Religion*, Volume 2, pp. 277-281 (New York, 1987).

5. The most influential exponent of this theory has been Helmut Hoffman in *The Religions of Tibet* (London, 1961) and *Tibet: A Handbook* (Bloomington, Indiana, 1975). His position has been criticized by Per Kværne, "Aspects of the Origin of the Buddhist Tradition in Tibet," *Numen*, 19 (1972) pp. 22-40.

6. The major work resulting from this collaboration is D.L. Snellgrove, *The Nine Ways of Bön* (London, 1967; reprint Boulder, Colorado, 1980).

7. A brief resumé of the biography of gShen-rab (based on the gZer-mig) may be found in Hoffman, *The Religions of Tibet*, pp. 85-95. A more detailed presentation is provided by Per Kværne, "Peintures tibétaines de la vie de sTonpa-gcen-rab," *Arts Asiatiques* 41 (1986) pp. 36-81, based on the gZi-brjid.

8. The history of Bön, as viewed by its own adherents, is dealt with in detail by S.G. Karmay, *The Treasury of Good Sayings: A Tibetan History of Bön* (London, 1972).

9. Krystyna Cech, "The History, Teaching and Practice of Dialectics according to the Bön Tradition," *The Tibet Journal* 11,2 (1986) pp. 3-28.

10. This ritual is discussed at length by R.A. Stein, "Le linga des danses masquées lamaïques et la théorie des âmes," *Sino-Indian Studies* 5, 3-4 (1957) pp. 200-234.

Glossary

baha	Nepalese monastery
bekhu	Chief
Bhotia	Tibetan living in Nepal
chang	Tibetan barley beer
chorpon	Guardian of a village temple
chorten	Buddhist shrine resembling the shape of a stupa
drawa	Buddhist monk
dukhang	Main hall of a Buddhist monastery
ger-pa	Social class of high status
gonpa	Tibetan Buddhist monastery
gyalpo	Chieftain equal to a raja
Khampa	Tibetan warrior tribe
Khashag	Tibetan cabinet appointed by the Dalai Lama
konier	Sacristan serving in Buddhist temple
kor-k'ong	Group meeting at festivals
kurim	Buddhist prayer intent on attaining practical advantage
ku-d'rag	Social class of high status
lhakhang	Temple or chapel
lyonpo	Cabinet minister of a district in Tibet
Mani-Rimdu	Buddhist ritual including masked sacred dances performed by lamas
mani-wall	Wall of slates inscribed with Buddhist prayers
miser	Middle social class
ngag-pa	Priestly social class
non-thou	A large kin group
pembu	Chief or headman
ponpo	Chief or headman
rhü	Tibetan patrilineal clan
rinpoche	Honorific title for reincarnate lama, literally 'precious one'
sangha	Buddhist community
stupa	Buddhist shrine of bi-spherical shape
Thak Khola	Region of Nepal drained by the Khali Gandaki River
Thakali	Member of a tribe from Thak Khola region of northwestern Nepal
thanka	Buddhist scroll painting
thabzing	Chinese 'class struggle sessions' applied as punishment for political diversion
thonje	Group of families living in the same locality
torma	Sacrificial cake used in Buddhist ritual
trongba	Small nuclear family
tsampa	Barley which has been roasted before being milled
tsang	Family
tsog	Buddhist sacrificial rite
thuktro	Picnic assembling a large group
tulku	Lama recognized as a reincarnation
Udaya	Nepalese of mixed Newar and Tibetan parentage
Vajracarya	Newar Buddhist priest expert in tantric rituals
vihara	Buddhist monastery in Nepal
ya-wa	Low social class

The Author

CHRISTOPH VON FÜRER-HAIMENDORF was born in Austria and studied anthropology at the University of Vienna and the University of London. Coming to India in 1936, he began his career in anthropological field research with a study of one of the Naga tribes. He extended his studies to the the tribal populations of Hyderabad state, Orissa and Arunachal Pradesh, and authored several standard works of Indian anthropological literature including *The Chenchus, The Reddis of the Bison Hills, The Raj Gonds of Adilabad* and *The Apa Tanis and Their Neighbours.* He served with the Government of India in the North East Frontier Agency from 1944 to 1945, and later was Adviser for Tribes and Backward Classes to the Nizam's Government.

In 1951, he was appointed to the Chair of Asian Anthropology at the University of London where he then established the Department of Anthropology in the School of Oriental and African Studies. Professor Haimendorf concentrated on the study of the hill people of Nepal from 1953 to 1983, and laid the foundation for the anthropological exploration of Nepal with his book *The Sherpas of Nepal, Caste and Kin in Nepal, India and Ceylon* and *Himalayan Traders.*

Since his retirement in 1976, he has continued his studies of tribal groups of India and Nepal, and authored numerous articles and books including *The Sherpas Transformed* and *The Renaissance of Tibetan Civilization* which documents the rebuilding of Tibetan culture in India and Nepal since the Chinese invasion of Tibet in 1959.

The Biosphere Catalogue
Editor: T. Parrish Snyder

The Biosphere Catalogue brings together state of the art information by leading scientists and thinkers in the various spheres of the biosphere — biomes, atmosphere, geosphere, evolution, communication, analytics, cities, travel, and more. ($12.95)

Space Biospheres
John Allen and Mark Nelson

Commencing with a brilliant and concise integrative model of the Earth's biosphere, the authors proceed to the modelling of Biosphere II, an extraordinary project in the creation of biospheric systems to further humankind's ability to live in harmony with the sphere of life — on Earth or among the stars. Revised second edition. ($8.95)

The Biosphere
Vladimir Vernadsky

The first English publication of the original theory of the biosphere written in 1926. Preface by Dr. Evgenii Shepelev from the Institute of Biomedical Problems, Moscow. ($5.95)

Traces of Bygone Biospheres
Andrey Lapo

The role of life in geological processes is revealed via the study of biomineralization and biosedimentation in the Earth's crust — the traces of bygone biospheres. ($9.95)

Where the Gods Reign:
Plants and Peoples of the Colombian Amazon Richard E. Schultes

Journey the mysterious Colombian Amazon with a most remarkable scientist and eloquent guide. With 140 black and white photographs from 1940-1954, Dr. Schultes presents an exquisite and moving portrait of his historic studies of ethnobotany in this remote region. ($20.00)

White Gold: *Diary of a Rubber Cutter in the Amazon 1906-1916*
John C. Yungjohann · Edited by Ghillean T. Prance

The exotic beauty, wildlife, plants and peoples of the Brazilian Amazon at the turn of the century come to life in this fascinating tale by a young man who survived the notorious tactics of the rubber barons through his friendship with the native peoples who taught him how to live in the rainforest. Edited and with introduction by one of the world's foremost tropical rainforest botanists. ($7.95)

SP
SYNERGETIC PRESS

Post Office Box 689 Oracle, Arizona 85623